CRIME VICTIM'S GUIDE TO JUSTICE

CRIME VICTIM'S GUIDE TO JUSTICE

Second Edition

——

Mary L. Boland
Attorney at Law

SPHINX® PUBLISHING
AN IMPRINT OF SOURCEBOOKS, INC.®
NAPERVILLE, ILLINOIS

Second Edition, 2001

Published by: **Sphinx® Publishing, An Imprint of Sourcebooks, Inc.®**

Naperville Office
P.O. Box 4410
Naperville, Illinois 60567-4410
630-961-3900
Fax: 630-961-2168
http://www.sourcebooks.com

This publication is designed to provide accurate and authoritative information in regard to the subject matter covered. It is sold with the understanding that the publisher is not engaged in rendering legal, accounting, or other professional service. If legal advice or other expert assistance is required, the services of a competent professional person should be sought.

From a Declaration of Principles Jointly Adopted by a Committee of the American Bar Association and a Committee of Publishers and Associations

This product is not a substitute for legal advice.

Disclaimer required by Texas statutes.

Library of Congress Cataloging-in-Publication Data
Boland, Mary L.
   Crime victim's guide to justice / Mary L. Boland.-- 2nd ed.
      p. cm. -- (Legal survival guides)
   Includes index.
   ISBN 1-57248-163-3
   1. Victims of crimes--Legal status, laws, etc.--United States--Popular works. 2. Criminal procedure--United States--Popular works. I. Title. II. Series.

KF9763.Z9 B65 2001
344.73'03288--dc21

                                                              2001041177

Printed and bound in the United States of America.

VHG Paperback — 10 9 8 7 6 5 4 3 2 1

CONTENTS

ACKNOWLEDGMENT

Many people contributed over several years to the information which eventually made its way into this book. I most want to thank Katherine A. Newell, an excellent paralegal and researcher, for her time and invaluable assistance in gathering, typing, and editing the compilation of statutory materials cited in the first edition of this book.

Using Self-Help
Law Books

Before using a self-help law book, you should realize the advantages and disadvantages of doing your own legal work and understand the challenges and diligence that this requires.

The Growing Trend

Rest assured that you won't be the first or only person handling your own legal matter. For example, in some states, more than seventy-five percent of divorces and other cases have at least one party representing him or herself. Because of the high cost of legal services, this is a major trend and many courts are struggling to make it easier for people to represent themselves. However, some courts are not happy with people who do not use attorneys and refuse to help them in any way. For some, the attitude is, "Go to the law library and figure it out for yourself."

We at Sphinx write and publish self-help law books to give people an alternative to the often complicated and confusing legal books found in most law libraries. We have made the explanations of the law as simple and easy to understand as possible. Of course, unlike an attorney advising an individual client, we cannot cover every conceivable possibility.

Cost/Value Analysis

Whenever you shop for a product or service, you are faced with various levels of quality and price. In deciding what product or service to buy, you make a cost/value analysis on the basis of your willingness to pay and the quality you desire.

When buying a car, you decide whether you want transportation, comfort, status, or sex appeal. Accordingly, you decide among such choices as a Neon, a Lincoln, a Rolls Royce, or a Porsche. Before making a decision, you usually weigh the merits of each option against the cost.

When you get a headache, you can take a pain reliever (such as aspirin) or visit a medical specialist for a neurological examination. Given this choice, most people, of course, take a pain reliever, since it costs only pennies; whereas a medical examination costs hundreds of dollars and takes a lot of time. This is usually a logical choice because it is rare to need anything more than a pain reliever for a headache. But in some cases, a headache may indicate a brain tumor and failing to see a specialist right away can result in complications. Should everyone with a headache go to a specialist? Of course not, but people treating their own illnesses must realize that they are betting on the basis of their cost/value analysis of the situation. They are taking the most logical option.

The same cost/value analysis must be made when deciding to do one's own legal work. Many legal situations are very straight forward, requiring a simple form and no complicated analysis. Anyone with a little intelligence and a book of instructions can handle the matter without outside help.

But there is always the chance that complications are involved that only an attorney would notice. To simplify the law into a book like this, several legal cases often must be condensed into a single sentence or paragraph. Otherwise, the book would be several hundred pages long and too complicated for most people. However, this simplification necessarily leaves out many details and nuances that would apply to special or unusual situations. Also, there are many ways to interpret most legal questions. Your case may come before a judge who disagrees with the analysis of our authors.

Therefore, in deciding to use a self-help law book and to do your own legal work, you must realize that you are making a cost/value analysis. You have decided that the money you will save in doing it yourself outweighs the chance that your case will not turn out to your satisfaction. Most people handling their own simple legal matters never have a problem, but occasionally people find that it ended up costing them more to have an attorney straighten out the situation than it would have if they had hired an attorney in the beginning. Keep this in mind if you decide to handle your own case, and be sure to consult an attorney if you feel you might need further guidance.

LOCAL RULES   The next thing to remember is that a book which covers the law for the entire nation, or even for an entire state, cannot possibly include every procedural difference of every county court. Whenever possible, we provide the exact form needed; however, in some areas, each county, or even each judge, may require unique forms and procedures. In our *state* books, our forms usually cover the majority of counties in the state, or provide examples of the type of form that will be required. In our *national* books, our forms are sometimes even more general in nature but are designed to give a good idea of the type of form that will be needed in most locations. Nonetheless, keep in mind that your *state*, county, or judge may have a requirement, or use a form, that is not included in this book.

You should not necessarily expect to be able to get all of the information and resources you need solely from within the pages of this book. This book will serve as your guide, giving you specific information whenever possible and helping you to find out what else you will need to know. This is just like if you decided to build your own backyard deck. You might purchase a book on how to build decks. However, such a book would not include the building codes and permit requirements of every city, town, county, and township in the nation; nor would it include the lumber, nails, saws, hammers, and other materials and tools you would need to actually build the deck. You would use the book as your guide, and then do some work and research involving such matters as whether you need a permit of some kind, what type and grade of wood are available in your area, whether to use hand tools or power tools, and how to use those tools.

Before using the forms in a book like this, you should check with your court clerk to see if there are any local rules of which you should be aware, or local forms you will need to use. Often, such forms will require the same information as the forms in the book but are merely laid out differently, use slightly different language, or use different color paper so the clerks can easily find them. They will sometimes require additional information.

CHANGES IN THE LAW

Besides being subject to local rules and practices, the law is subject to change at any time. The courts and the legislatures of all fifty states are constantly revising the laws. It is possible that while you are reading this book, some aspect of the law is being changed.

In most cases, the change will be of minimal significance. A form will be redesigned, additional information will be required, or a waiting period will be extended. As a result, you might need to revise a form, file an extra form, or wait out a longer time period; these types of changes will not usually affect the outcome of your case. On the other hand, sometimes a major part of the law is changed, the entire law in a particular area is rewritten, or a case that was the basis of a central legal point is overruled. In such instances, your entire ability to pursue your case may be impaired.

To help you with local requirements and changes in the law, be sure to review Appendix B on "Legal Research."

Again, you should weigh the value of your case against the cost of an attorney and make a decision as to what you believe is in your best interest.

INTRODUCTION

Nearly everyone will be affected by crime in some way during their lifetime. Television brings trials into our homes, and "court-watching" has become commonplace. Yet, beyond the media hype, a victim's rights are a mystery to most, and no one can exercise rights they do not know exist. Victims, their families, and supporters must learn about these laws and learn how and when to apply this knowledge.

This book will help you understand the criminal and civil court systems from the victim's perspective. It is intended to teach you how the criminal justice system functions, what your rights are as a victim, how to find help, and how to make the people who make the decisions about your case accountable to you. This book is also intended to help victims who are considering filing a civil lawsuit. It is a starting place, a basic guide to the maze of our civil court process.

Do not hesitate to demand justice as you travel from victim to survivor. And when your journey is complete, gather strength from your experience and think about how you can have an impact on your community to improve the treatment of future victims.

Chapters 1 through 17 discuss the criminal court process. Chapters 18 through 20 explain the civil court process, and other ways to go about obtaining compensation for your losses due to being a crime victim. The glossary will help you understand the legal jargon used in all the chapters. Most italicized words throughout the text are in the glossary.

Appendix A lists street and Internet addresses and telephone numbers that may be useful to you.

Appendix B provides some basic information about legal research, in the event you want to go beyond what is covered in this book.

Appendix C gives information about the laws of each state relating to crime victims.

Appendix D contains examples of letters and forms. These either illustrate the type of forms you may encounter as a crime victim or the type of forms you may find helpful to secure your rights.

THE CRIMINAL JUSTICE SYSTEM

1

In colonial times, when a person committed a crime, it was considered to be an injury to the victim and the victim was entitled to prosecute the case. This system favored wealthy victims, however, because poorer victims did not have the financial resources to seek justice. To make the process fairer, the government took over the responsibility of prosecuting a person accused of committing a crime. Crimes began to be considered public wrongs committed against the community, rather than private wrongs committed only against the individual victim.

THE LAW

There are federal laws and procedures that apply to cases prosecuted in the federal court system, but most crimes are prosecuted in the state court systems. Within constitutional limits, each state is free to enact its own criminal laws and procedural rules, and has the right to develop its own descriptions, definitions, and classification of crimes. For example, what is called "rape" in one state may be called "sexual battery" or "sexual assault" by another. Where three people held up at gunpoint while the perpetrator empties the cash register is considered a single robbery in one state, it may be considered three robberies in another. The theft of $50 may be a misdemeanor in one state, and a felony in another.

THE SYSTEM

The criminal justice system is designed to deter the commission of crimes, investigate and prosecute crimes, and punish and attempt to rehabilitate convicted offenders. The "system" refers to a group of agencies that have responsibility for taking action at certain times in the case. The *police* take the report and investigate the crime. The *prosecutor* charges the accused and tries the case. The *judge* oversees the court process. *Corrections personnel* are responsible for the incarceration of the defendant. Each of these agencies is separate, and each has a different goal and purpose. Sometimes they do not work well together; however, in recent years, police and prosecutors have joined together to form task forces or specialized units to improve the handling of certain types of cases.

TYPES OF CRIMES

The most common classifications of crime in the United States are *misdemeanors* and *felonies*. Each state can determine which crimes are felonies and which are misdemeanors. One common method of categorizing crimes is by the length of sentence. The least serious crimes are called *petty offenses* or *infractions* in most states. Examples of typical petty offenses are:

- traffic violations;

- disturbing the peace; and

- loitering.

In most states the maximum sentence for a misdemeanor is one year, although a few permit two years. Examples of typical misdemeanors are:

- assault;

- simple theft;

- trespass;

- battery;

- public indecency (exposure); and

- telephone harassment.

A felony is a more serious crime, and can be punishable by longer prison terms, a life sentence, or even death. Examples of typical felonies are:

- murder;

- rape and sexual assault;

- arson;

- forgery;

- drugs (certain kinds);

- manslaughter;

- home invasion;

- carjacking;

- theft (over a certain amount); and

- aggravated stalking.

ELEMENTS OF CRIMES

In order to constitute a crime, certain *elements* must be present. These will be stated in the laws.

Example: A traditional first-degree murder requires proof of four elements:

(1) killing a person;

(2) unlawfully (without a legally justifiable excuse);

(3) intentionally; and

(4) with malice aforethought (i.e., with prior planning).

If one or more of the elements is not present, it is not sufficient to charge the offense, although it may be possible to charge another lesser offense.

Example: If the killing was *unlawful* (unauthorized) and *intentional* (not an accident), but *malice aforethought* (prior planning) was not present, it might still be charged as a lesser offense of second degree murder.

Every crime has its own definition. An example of a criminal statute in Illinois defining the offense of residential burglary follows:

```
A person commits residential burglary who
knowingly and without authority enters the
dwelling place of another with the intent to
commit therein a felony or theft.
```

The definition of *dwelling* is found at another section of Illinois' criminal code:

```
For the purposes of Section 19-3 of this
Code, "dwelling" means a house, apartment,
mobile home, trailer, or other living quar-
ters in which at the time of the alleged
offense, the owners or occupants actually
reside or in their absence intend within a
reasonable period of time to reside.
```

Thus, sometimes, in order to fully understand the required elements of an offense, research may disclose more than one statute or section of law.

THE OFFENDER

Once a person is accused of a crime, he or she becomes a party to the case and is entitled to the protection of the United States Constitution, and all laws that apply to persons charged with a crime. Everyone who participates in committing the crime can be charged with the offense.

Example: If three carjackers steal your car, each can be charged even if only one has the gun or drives away. The others can be held to be accountable for the actions of the gun-wielding driver.

An example of an *accountability* statute is:

A person is legally accountable for the conduct of another in Illinois when:

> Either before or during the commission of an offense, and with the intent to promote or facilitate such commission, he solicits, aids, abets, agrees or attempts to aid, such other person in the planning or commission of the offense.

JUVENILES

Teenage and younger offenders are responsible for a large percentage of the crimes committed in the United States today. Until recently, however, juveniles who committed crimes were considered *delinquent* and sent to a special juvenile court for processing. Most state laws still only permit criminal convictions against older teen offenders on the theory that younger children are not fully responsible for their conduct. Some states do permit transfer to an adult court of a juvenile who commits a particularly violent or brutal crime.

FAMILY
MEMBERS

Family members can, and do, commit crimes against one another. Most often, the crimes of violence are called *domestic violence*, but family members commit a range of criminal acts against one another. Technically, the criminal law does not distinguish between a family member offender and a stranger, but in fact, the criminal justice system seems to treat crimes committed by family members as being less serious. For many years, the criminal justice system treated crimes between family members as private disputes, and not public wrongs. Concepts of "private family matters" sometimes do affect charging decisions and sentencing options for family member offenders.

THE STATE'S CASE

In our system of justice, a criminal defendant is always presumed innocent. Therefore, in all cases, the state has the entire *burden of proving* through the introduction of testimony or physical evidence at trial "beyond a reasonable doubt" that a crime was committed and that the defendant committed the crime. The defense has no *burden of proof* in a criminal case. (The defense does not even have to prove innocence.) The Fifth Amendment to the U.S. Constitution guarantees that the defendant cannot be made to *incriminate* (testify against) him or herself. That is why the defendant does not have to testify.

In the majority of cases, the *testimony* of a single witness is legally sufficient to convict a defendant in a criminal case.

Even *circumstantial evidence* may be sufficient to convict a defendant. But, because judges and juries want to have as much evidence as possible before convicting, often the state will introduce physical and scientific evidence in addition to the testimony of the victim and other witnesses.

Scientific evidence, such as DNA, is being used today in many cases. DNA is short for deoxyribonucleic acid and can provide physical evidence (such as that found in saliva, blood, or other bodily fluids) that a person was at the crime scene.

THE DEFENSE CASE

When a *defendant* is charged with a crime, he or she may be entitled to an appointed attorney as guaranteed by the Sixth Amendment. In all cases, a defendant with the financial resources can hire an attorney. The defense attorney is present to insure that a defendant's rights are not violated. The goal of the defense is to obtain a dismissal or acquittal whenever possible. The strategies used will vary depending on the kind of case, but will generally be as follows:

- the evidence is insufficient;

- the state violated the defendant's rights in gathering the evidence;

- the witnesses cannot be believed;

- consent or fabrication;

- mistaken identity;

- self defense;

- entrapment or involuntary act; or

- the defendant is unfit, insane, or guilty but mentally ill.

INSUFFICIENT
EVIDENCE

The defense may argue that the evidence is insufficient where there is little physical evidence, like fingerprints, to connect the defendant to the crime, and where the witnesses may have had little opportunity to observe the defendant.

VIOLATED
RIGHTS

Even where there is strong physical evidence, like a match between the defendant's blood and blood collected at the scene, the defendant may argue that the state violated the defendant's rights in gathering the evidence. In this kind of case, the defense may also attack the police investigation techniques, or the crime lab's processing and analyzing of the evidence.

UNBELIEVABILITY

The defense may be that the victim cannot be believed. This defense is commonly seen where there are few witnesses other than the victim of the crime. The defendant attacks the motives of the victim in reporting the crime or in identifying the defendant.

Example: The defendant might argue that the victim made up the story of the assault or battery to avoid getting into trouble for coming home late. Another defendant might claim that the victim wanted the insurance money for an item of property that was reported stolen.

CONSENT OR
FABRICATION

In sexual assault cases, where the defendant is an acquaintance of the victim, he may admit the sexual acts, but contend that the victim agreed to have sex. This *consent* defense attacks the believability of the victim and is often used where there is a lack of evidence of bruising or other injury to the victim. If the victim is a child, the defendant in this type of case will typically argue *fabrication* by the child due to immaturity or coaching by some adult.

MISTAKEN
IDENTITY

Mistaken identity is often claimed by defendants when the victim is physically injured or where the defendant is a stranger. This defense questions the victim's memory and accuracy of identification. Today, scientific improvements like fingerprinting and DNA (deoxyribonucleic acid) genetic matching techniques have made it easier to identify stranger-defendants, but the mistaken identity defense is still raised where there is a lack of scientific evidence.

SELF DEFENSE

In bodily harm, physical assault, or battery cases, the defendant may claim self defense. Most states require the defendant to have acted on a reasonable belief that the conduct was necessary to avoid imminent physical harm or death, but the unreasonableness of a defendant's belief does not seem to deter claims of self defense.

Example: An Illinois newspaper reported that when a 200 lb. man was arrested for the murder of his 110 lb. co-worker, he claimed he stabbed her to death in self defense after she tried to "force" him to have sex in the parking garage on their way to work.

ENTRAPMENT

A defendant may also claim *entrapment* as a defense. This is common in drug cases where the defendant contends that the police enticed or lured the defendant into committing the criminal acts. Another defense, involuntariness, might be seen in gang or multiple-offender cases where the defendant argues that he or she was forced by the other defendants to go along and commit the crime.

INSANITY

One of the required elements for a criminal charge is the ability to form a criminal intent. When a defendant is incapacitated, unfit, or insane, he or she may claim that they lacked the necessary mental state to commit the crime or to stand trial for committing the crime. All states have procedures for determining fitness and sanity. These hearings will require expert psychiatric evaluation and testimony, and may result in deferral of prosecution for some period of time. If such an option is not available, there may be a finding of dangerousness or insanity, and a proceeding to commit the defendant into a mental health facility for treatment until he or she is no longer dangerous or insane. Such a defendant is then subject to release under the state's mental health code.

In some states, "guilty but mentally ill" is permitted as a method of responding to some of these criminals. A finding of guilty but mentally ill permits incarcerating these offenders in mental health facilities for the duration of their mental illness, then transferring them to prison for the remainder of their sentences..

TEMPORARY
INSANITY

Temporary insanity may be raised as a defense where a defendant claims that he or she was insane at the time the crime was committed and therefore should not be held responsible for it. The "twinkie defense" in which the defendant claimed that high levels of blood sugar caused the crime and other "diminished capacity" defenses are similar type of claims. In these defenses, the defendant has "recovered" shortly after the crime, but nonetheless seeks to excuse his or her actions on the theory that they did not have the necessary criminal intent to commit their crime.

SURVIVING THE SYSTEM

In the past 20 years, the National Crime Survey has recorded more than 119 million violent crimes including rape, robbery, or assault. The latest National Crime Victimization Survey conducted by the U.S. Department of Justice, reported that there were nearly 11 million violent crimes and 31 million property crimes committed in the U.S. in 1994. These crimes included 2.5 million aggravated assaults, more than 400,000 rapes and sexual assaults, and 23,000 homicides.

The numbers improved in the past few years, but according to the FBI Crime Clock for 1999: one violent crime occurred every 22 seconds; one murder every 34 minutes; one forcible rape every 6 minutes; one robbery every minute; and one aggravated assault every 34 seconds. (Federal Bureau of Investigation (FBI). October 15, 2000. Crime in the

United States, Uniform Crime Reports, 1999. Washington, DC: U.S. Department of Justice.)

While males have the highest rate of victimization, rates for males are declining. Rates for women (more than 4.7 million crimes annually) have remained constant or are increasing. Men are more likely to face victimization by a stranger; women are as likely to be attacked by an acquaintance. In addition, hundreds of thousands of children are victimized every year in the United States, usually by someone they know.

The reality is that anyone can become a victim. And being the victim of a crime is just the beginning of a long and difficult journey in the criminal justice system.

THE IMPACT OF CRIME

Not all crimes are alike, nor are all victims affected the same way by crime, but most victims do experience some sense of loss as a result of crime. Victims may have physical, emotional, and psychological injuries, as well as loss of property. Even if the crime perpetrated against you or your loved one is relatively minor from the standpoint of the legal system, it may have a profound impact on you.

Many victims report feeling powerless, fearful, guilty, confused, and angry. Realize that recovering from the crime may take some time. Short term crisis intervention will help, but it may take a year or longer to regain a sense of normalcy in your life. You may feel overwhelmed by the crime against you and may not think you have enough energy to fight for your rights, but there are ways.

GETTING HELP 2

There are many avenues that victims can look to for support. If you have a religious or spiritual advisor, check with them for resources. Sometimes a friend can offer rest, comfort, and assistance, but often friends and family members need help understanding the crime or the criminal justice system themselves and may not be able to offer much help. The services of a psychiatrist, psychologist, psychotherapist, or counselor may better suit your needs. The title of the helper is not as important as whether that person is competent to deal with your specific kind of case.

Make sure you ask about credentials and experience in handling cases like yours. Talk with the person and then make your decision. Meeting with a trained person who can help you make sense of what you are feeling can also help you gather the strength you need to stay and fight for your rights.

In 1984, the Federal Government passed the Victims of Crime Act, which provides funding to the states to develop and initiate programs for crime victims. Today, many states have funded programs that provide information, counseling, and advocacy to crime victims. These programs can provide you with crisis intervention through hotlines, explain financial procedures, help acquaint you with court procedures, and provide information on local shelters and centers.

VICTIM-ASSISTANCE PROGRAMS

Victim-assistance personnel act as a liaison between the victim and the criminal justice system, and their services are free of charge. Many larger police departments and prosecutor's offices employ victim-assistance, also called victim-witness, personnel. Because these programs are funded locally, they may be very thorough and comprehensive, or they may be limited to providing information only. Usually, at a minimum, these persons can help to explain local procedures and will often have local resource information for your referral.

HOTLINE SERVICES

Some public or private agencies have established *hotlines* to assist crime victims. These phone lines may operate 24-hours a day and are usually called *crisis* lines. Often, a trained staff member or volunteer can help ease your immediate concerns over the phone and set up an appointment for you to see a counselor or refer you to another resource. These hotlines may also be set up for information and referral only. Many hotlines do provide confidentiality, but before leaving any identifying information, make sure you understand what kind of confidentiality is offered by the hotline service.

CRISIS COUNSELING

Many states also provide funding for agencies to provide some counseling and peer support to victims of crime. Rape crisis centers and domestic violence shelters are a few examples. Many programs also serve the families and significant others of the victims.

Programs may offer a number of free counseling sessions for victims and significant others, or may charge according to a sliding fee scale, based on your ability to pay. The programs may also run support groups for victims to join together and talk about their situations. If you do choose a program that has a charge, remember that you may be able to file an insurance claim or seek reimbursement through your state's crime victim compensation program, so keep a record of your billing.

Many crime victims are concerned about their privacy rights when they share intimate fears and details of the crime with a counselor or in a support group. In recognition of the victim's privacy concerns, some states provide legal protection for victim's privacy rights, and counseling programs are often available on a confidential basis. Before you choose, make sure you understand what kind of confidentiality is available through that person or agency.

THE CRIME VICTIM ADVOCATE

A *crime victim's advocate* is a person who can provide information, assistance, and referral services. Some can provide services immediately after the crime, such as rape victim advocates who go to the hospital with the victim. Advocates can be volunteers or staff members of large or small private or public agencies. Most have attended some kind of training on court systems and processes and should be able to provide you with information on the procedures that will apply to your case.

FINDING A PROGRAM

Finding a program has been made much easier with the advent of the Internet, because many government and community agencies now have websites. Many also provide excellent links to other sites that provide crime victims with information. Not all programs are on the Internet, but most nonprofit crime victim organizations obtain some state or federal funding in addition to private resources. Each state has an administrator for the federal funds, and this agency will have a listing of the programs that receive funding to provide crime victim assistance. Many private and public programs advertise or network with their local police or prosecutor, and they will be able to refer you for help.

If you have checked your local resources—police, prosecutors, the yellow pages, the library, city hall—and cannot find a local program, look for a statewide listing of victim service programs. Sometimes, a state agency or organization can provide assistance even if they are not based in your town or county. Contacting your attorney general's office can also be useful, since many of them have victim service information. Finally, your state representative or senator may have information to assist you in finding a local chapter of a statewide network.

No Local Programs

Some jurisdictions have not yet established formal programs to help victims. If you have no luck in finding a program, there may nonetheless be an informal group that meets. Ask your local police officer or prosecutor for assistance in finding such a group. In Appendix A of this book you will find selected national agencies that may also be able to assist you in finding a local resource.

The Victim in the Criminal Justice System

3

Even though the crime is committed against the victim, the victim is often seen as peripheral to the case. The victim is not a party to the case, and cannot force the prosecutor to act on his or her behalf. The law does not permit a victim to privately prosecute a criminal case. For many years, victims did not have any rights. They were expected to appear and give testimony, often without much preparation from the prosecutor. It may take months, even years, for a case to come to trial, and many victims just dropped out of the criminal court process.

But victims are essential to successfully prosecuting a case, and during the 1960s and 1970s, victim's rights groups began to be heard by the criminal justice system. Eventually, every state passed laws giving victims some rights to information and participation in the case. But sometimes times, the agencies required to provide victims with rights fail to do so. As a result, most victims remain unaware of their rights to participate in the case, so they do not demand it.

FAMILY MEMBERS AND LOVED ONES

The attack on the victim will often have serious consequences for the victim's loved ones. Anger and disbelief are common feelings. When a victim is killed as a result of the crime, the family and loved ones often suffer severe emotional, and even physical, effects from the crime.

For many years, these family members and loved ones did not have a role in the criminal justice system. In most cases, they are not witnesses and so cannot testify. They were not given notices of court hearings and often did not know exactly what was happening in the case. They were not asked how they felt to have a *plea bargain* struck, and they sometimes did not even know the sentence at all. (A plea bargain is where the defendant is allowed to plead guilty to some or all of the charges, often in return for the state's recommendation of a particular sentence, which is likely to be lower than if the defendant went to trial.)

Today, this has changed and if a victim dies, the family or a designated person steps into the victim's shoes and has the rights granted to the victim in that state or jurisdiction. Thus, if your family member or loved one was killed, you become the "victim" for purposes of notification and the right to participate in the criminal justice system.

WITNESSES

Witnesses have many of the same concerns about privacy and safety that victims have. In an effort to encourage witnesses to come forward and testify, the law has included witnesses in some of the protections given to crime victims.

THE GROWTH OF VICTIMS' RIGHTS

The first Presidential Task Force on Victims of Crime was established in the 1980s. Since then, there have been evolving improvements for crime victims.

RAPE EVIDENCE
COLLECTION KITS

Before the Presidential Task Force changed medical protocols, rape was not considered an injury by many hospitals. *Rape evidence collection kits* and the training of hospital staff are modifications that have improved the experiences of the victim. The kits standardized the type and quantity of evidence collected, so that all medical procedures and evidentiary requirements could be completed in most cases at the initial emergency room visit.

Also, training of medical personnel improved the understanding of the dynamics of certain kinds of crimes, which resulted in more sensitive treatment of victims. For example, prior to training, some medical personnel blamed domestic violence victims for the crimes, asking "why didn't you leave, if this has happened before?" or "what were you two fighting about this time?" This made victims more reluctant to report the true nature of the injury. Some preferred to say that they had "fallen down stairs," or "bumped into a door," rather than be humiliated with questions or comments from medical staff. Training on the dynamics of domestic violence, including the cycle of violence often present in these cases, improved the treatment of the victim and made victims more likely to report the crimes.

PUBLIC
RECORDS

Prior to the changes in the law, the victim's name and address were available as public records. As a result, victims were easily accessible to harassment by the media, insurance and security salesmen, and the perpetrator of the crime. Today, release of the victim's address on public records may be prohibited. Some states also provide victims with protection from the assailant's intimidation by adding new crimes for communication or harassment of a witness, and increasing penalties for offenders who harass witnesses prior to trial. In some states, the offender's bail may be revoked if he or she violates the condition prohibiting him or her from contacting the victim pending trial, and he or she could return to jail until trial.

BAIL
CONDITIONS

After being arrested, some offenders continue to harass their victim, either from a jail phone or after being released on bail (often without the victim being made aware of the release). When releasing the accused on *bail*, judges were not always aware of continued threats or harassment of the victim. Today, prosecutors more often confer with victims regarding danger issues and bail conditions. In some states, information about bail release is available, and intimidation of the victim may specifically be cause for the revocation of bail.

PRELIMINARY
HEARING

Prior to changes in the law, no one would tell the victim what was involved in a preliminary hearing, how long it would take, or how they should prepare. Now, victims are entitled to know about the procedures. Prosecutors and victim-witness personnel take the time to prepare the victim.

NOTE: *In order to avoid overzealous defense investigators, the state of Oregon gives victims a constitutional right to refuse to speak with defense investigators.*

Victims and assailants often came in contact with each other in the hallways surrounding the preliminary hearings, causing the victim continued distress. Victims are now entitled to wait in areas that minimize contact with the defendant.

CONTINUANCES Repeated continuances can cost the victim unnecessary expenses such as hiring a baby-sitter, leave from work, and parking. Some states require the judge to consider the impact of continuances on a victim. (Ohio even permits the victim to object.)

TESTIMONY Prior to 1982, refusing to disclose your home and work address could result in being held in contempt of court. In order to maintain the privacy of the victim, some states prohibit compelling a victim to testify as to their address and other identifying information unless there is a valid legal reason.

Testifying can be a terrifying experience, especially to a child. Certain victims may now have a support person present in court; child victims may be entitled to specialized consideration.

PROSECUTORS Prosecutors could be repeatedly reassigned before the trial begins. Victims would have to tell each new prosecutor the detailed story and would not receive notification of continuances. As a result of new laws, some prosecutor's offices have a single prosecutor stay with the case from start to finish in certain kinds of felonies. Victims are also entitled to information on continuances.

Because of these improvements, initiated since the 1982 task force report, victims now have some legal rights in the criminal justice system that did not exist just over a decade ago.

CONSTITUTIONAL RIGHTS OF VICTIMS

The most important right that one can hold under the criminal justice system is a *constitutional right*. Defendants have had them since the founding of our country, but even though the President's Task Force recommended the addition of a Crime Victim's Amendment as long ago as 1982, victim's rights are still not in the U.S. Constitution. Instead, many states have passed state constitutional amendments that grant victims the right to be treated with fairness and dignity in their state's criminal justice system. The state listings in Appendix B will tell you if your state has such a constitutional amendment or provision.

If your state has a crime victims' constitutional amendment, your next step is to get a copy. Since most amendments have been passed within the past few years, be sure to get the most current revision of your state's constitution. The attorney general of your state will be able to supply you with a copy of your state constitution. Any public library that has a current copy of your state constitution should have a copy of the amendment. (The Amendment may also be listed on the Internet.) Even if your state does not yet have a constitutional provision, all states have passed laws giving crime victims some statutory rights. For more on how to find the laws in your state, see Appendix B on legal research tips and the listing for your state in Appendix C.

VICTIM "BILL OF RIGHTS" LAWS

By 1990, every state passed victim rights laws. Most are called *"bill of rights"* acts. Many of the laws apply to cases prosecuted in both criminal and juvenile courts, and some states include certain specified misdemeanor and vehicular crimes. Family members or close relatives may be designated to participate on behalf of a minor, incapacitated, or deceased victim. In some states, the victim is permitted to designate another person to exercise the victim's rights. Typically, the laws provide victims with the right to information, participation, and services.

RIGHT TO INFORMATION

Most states provide that victims are to be informed of their role, general procedures, and the medical, social, and financial services available to victims. Some states have produced form notices, which police give to victims at their first contact. The victim may be provided with a name, address, and contact phone number of the police officer or prosecutor assigned to the case. Larger police departments may have victim-assistance officers who keep the victim informed as to the status of the case and provide any notices or written follow-up to the victim on victim assistance programs, such as available crisis intervention or crime victims' compensation (sometimes called *reparation*).

Although some information may be automatically provided, states commonly require the victim to request to be kept informed of case progress. Send letters to the police and prosecutor requesting to be kept informed. These letters also serve to keep officials informed of your address and other contact information. (For a sample letter to police and prosecutor, see form A in Appendix D.) Case information may include the status of the investigation, arrest, release of the accused on bail, filing of charges (or decision not to file), commencement of prosecution, hearings and continuances, sentencing date, and judge's decision or judgment of conviction and release of the offender.

RIGHT TO
PARTICIPATION

The role of the victim in the criminal justice system is expanding, and victims are entitled to participate in criminal proceedings in virtually every state. In some states, the victim is permitted to present testimony at the bail hearing regarding fear of harm or threats by the defendant. In others, the prosecutor is required to confer or consult with the victim prior to making charging decisions.

In many states, the victim is now entitled to be present at court proceedings on the same basis as the defendant. In some states, the victim's welfare is considered in determining whether continuances will be granted, and one state (Ohio) permits the victim to object to a continuance request. A few states also permit the victim to bring a support person into court while the victim testifies.

Perhaps the most critical phase of a criminal case for the victim is the sentencing decision, and all states permit some victim input into consideration of the sentence. Because the vast majority of criminal cases are resolved by plea bargain, the sentencing hearing will be the only opportunity for the victim to speak to the judge about the crime. In many states, the prosecutor is required to consult with the victim prior to plea negotiations or agreement (this does not mean that the victim can force the prosecutor to take any particular action, but only requires the prosecutor to consider the victim's position). Also, written *victim impact statements* are often included in the materials the judge considers prior to approving a plea or determining a sentence. In some states, the victim is entitled to present the statement in person and to recommend an appropriate sentence.

Victim impact information is also crucial in consideration of parole, pardon, or commutation of an offender's sentence, and many states permit written and oral presentation of a victim impact statement to parole officials. Victims are entitled to know if the offender escapes and if he or she is recaptured. In order to exercise this right, victims must keep corrections officials informed of their address. See form C in Appendix D for a sample letter to corrections officials.

FREEDOM FROM INTIMIDATION AND HARASSMENT

States expressly provide that victims be given information on the right to be free of intimidation while cooperating with law enforcement in the prosecution of their case. Secure or safe waiting areas are to be provided to victims while attending court proceedings to minimize their contact with the defendant and the defendant's family and friends. The police or other criminal justice personnel may provide protective assistance, and in all states, intimidation of the victim can be a criminal act. In some states, the prosecutor may specifically request revocation of the defendant's bond for intimidating, threatening, or harming the victim or the victim's family.

RETURN OF PROPERTY

Court procedures can be lengthy. Property taken as evidence or recovered by police in the possession of the offender should be promptly returned to the victim once its evidentiary purpose has been met. In some states, this means that once police photograph or the crime lab analyzes the materials, they should be returned to the victim. In a few states, officials are required to return property within 5-10 days after requested by the victim, unless good cause can be shown why the property cannot be returned.

THE RIGHT TO RESTITUTION

Some states make *restitution* mandatory, while others permit the victim to make a request for consideration by the court in the victim impact statement. For an explanation of restitution, see the section "Other Options for Recovery of Damages" in Chapter 17.

THE RIGHT TO COMPENSATION

Every state has passed a crime victim's compensation (reparation) law which provides victims with the right to seek compensation from the state for their monetary losses incurred as a result of the crime. Each state's requirements differ. For example, in one state the victim must report the crime to police within 72 hours. In other states, the law only applies to "violent" crimes. The Attorney General's Office of each state will be able to provide you with the necessary information on how and where to file for crime victim's compensation.

> ***Warning:*** Do not wait too long before investigating your rights as there are time limits within which you must file your claim. A state-by-state listing of agencies that can assist in filing compensation claims is in Appendix A.

THE RIGHT TO CIVIL JUSTICE

Every crime is a public wrong, but it is also a private wrong. Private, or *civil*, wrongs are called *torts*. The crime of battery, for example, is also a tort of battery. Torts are the basis for personal injury and property damage civil lawsuits. So, every crime victim is also entitled to file a civil lawsuit to seek money damages for the pain, suffering, and economic losses caused by the crime. Some states also permit victims to file civil restitution liens against the defendant, and to file claims for the offender's profits that he or she may make through selling the rights to his or her story, writing a book, or selling paintings as John Wayne Gacy did.

CASE MANAGEMENT

Criminal cases may take a long time to complete. Preparation includes organizing your materials so that you have ready access to important information which you may need as you travel through your case. You may also need this information for use in the civil case, or to check on the offender's release information. Organize material from the oldest (on the bottom or in the back) to the newest, and use folders or colored sheets to separate topics. The following suggestions will help you keep good records:

- Select a place to keep your records. Obtain a storage or moving box with a cover, a large file folder or 3-ring binder from an office supply store, or clear a space on your bookcase or in a drawer.

- Take every form, brochure, or informational sheet that is offered to you or that is available for victims of crime. Even if you are not sure that you may use the service listed, take it.

- When you are at the police station, or the hospital, ask for copies of brochures and other forms for crime victims.

- Contact your local crime victim's crisis center or resource center for information. Request that they send you any available information pertaining to your fact pattern.

- Put every sheet that pertains to crisis or emergency victim services on one file, section, or stack. You may need these hotline numbers in the middle of the night or during a crisis.

- Ask for a copy of your police report, and any other available law enforcement documents.

- Contact your local prosecutor's office or speak to victim-witness personnel for copies of charging documents and relevant laws.

- Check with your state attorney general's office for a victim's or crime bureau division, and ask them to send you copies of information on crime victim compensation and other programs for victims.

- Separate police, prosecutor, and legal information into separate stacks or files.

- Keep a log for each file. Every time you have a contact, write down the date, to whom you talked, and a brief description of the discussion.

- Take a notepad and pen with you when you meet with criminal justice officials and attend court proceedings. Be aware, however, that if you take notes into court with you, the defense attorney may want to examine them. Check with your prosecutor before you do so.

- Keep copies of letters you write to police, prosecutors, the judge, or corrections officials.

- Use a small calendar to keep track of events in your case. Carry it with you to all meetings and hearings, and write down any future or continuance dates.

- Use a small address book to keep the names, addresses, and phone numbers of police and prosecutors, judges, victim-assistance personnel, probation, corrections, and parole officers. Do not hesitate to request a name, address, and telephone number. Take a business card if one is available.

Throughout your case, update your records. There is no need to keep several copies of each item; one will do. By organizing your records, you will be able to utilize information in filing insurance claims or crime victim's compensation forms, during testimony, at sentencing and parole hearings, or for filing a later civil lien or a *civil suit*.

YOUR PRIVACY RIGHTS 4

The criminal justice system is generally open to the public. The concept of a public proceeding promotes fairness and openness in decision making. News media often assign reporters to cover police beats and trial dockets. Many people will recall the tremendous press coverage of well-known defendants, such as O.J. Simpson and Mike Tyson. The theory is that the public has the right to know what goes on in the courts in order to guard against government abuse that could occur if secret proceedings were permitted. In addition to the public's right to know, the press has a First Amendment right to obtain information and report on what goes on in the courts. But respecting the media's First Amendment rights can conflict with the profound impact that the crime has on a victim's sense of privacy, safety, and security. The public nature of criminal justice proceedings may intimidate some victims from seeking justice. Therefore, states have attempted to balance the privacy interests of victims with the openness of criminal proceedings.

PROTECTING THE VICTIM'S PRIVACY

During the 1980s, the growing victim's rights movements increased sensitivity to the issue of victim privacy. Some police routinely "blackout" identifying information from police reports. Since the press has usually obtained identifying information about the victim of a crime from police records, this can protect a victim from press scrutiny before trial. Also, some members of the press are sensitive to crime victims' privacy interests and may have an internal policy that prohibits printing a victim's name and address in certain kinds of cases, like sex crimes. (But in 1980, the United States Supreme Court decided that the First Amendment requires that in all but rare cases the criminal trial had to remain open to the public and the press.) Thus, once the case is filed, court documents with victim information become available to the press.

VICTIM INFORMATION

Some states have responded by enacting legislation that would prohibit police, prosecutors, or other public officials from releasing this information to the press. Thus, private identifying victim information does not become part of the public record. For example, Pennsylvania law provides that the victim's address and phone number shall not be disseminated to persons other than the police, prosecutor, or corrections officials without the consent of the victim.

TESTIMONY

There is also some protection for victims while testifying in open court. In some states, a victim cannot be compelled to testify as to his or her address or phone number. Ohio, for example, permits a prosecutor to seek a court order to protect the victim from being compelled to provide a home address, business address, phone numbers, or similar identifying information.

CAMERAS

Cameras have also invaded the courtrooms. By the end of 1991, 38 states permitted cameras in trial as well as appellate courts. In some states, only appellate courts permit cameras, but in others, like California, it is within the discretion of the trial judge to permit cameras in the courtroom. Some judges protect a victim's privacy by not permitting the cameras to show the victim's face while testifying.

YOUR RIGHTS AND THE MEDIA

The choice to speak to the media is the victim's. Sometimes reporters can become demanding, but a victim is never required to give any kind of statement to the press. On the other hand, some victims have chosen to publicize their cases in an effort to gain attention to the crime or their treatment, and media coverage can be a cathartic experience for some victims.

If you do choose to give an interview, remember that you have the right to refuse to answer any question or set limits on the areas of the interview. For example, you can choose the time and the place for the interview. You have the right to discuss with that reporter what the purpose of the interview is before the interview begins. You can also ask the reporter not to go into certain areas or show your face or present certain pictures. You can also choose to speak to a certain reporter, and just because you have spoken to one reporter, that does not mean that you must speak to any who approach you. You can also decide to stop speaking to reporters at any time. If you feel more comfortable, you can simply choose to release a statement in writing to the press.

For additional guidance and information, the National Center for Victims of Crime has developed guidelines for dealing with the press interviews and for being a guest on a talk show. See Appendix A for contact information.

REPORTING THE CRIME 5

Reporting the crime to police sets the criminal justice system in motion. An immediate report to police provides the best opportunity to apprehend the offender before crucial evidence is lost or destroyed. Prompt reporting is also important in prosecution.

Some victims immediately report the crime. In other cases, a passerby, eyewitness, friend, or family member calls the police. In cases of violence between acquaintances, domestic violence, rape, and child abuse, it is not unusual for the victim to wait hours, days, months, or even years before notifying police.

Although the police are primarily trained to investigate current reports of crime, many departments encourage citizens to report older cases as a way of solving repeat crimes. A criminal may continue to attack victims, developing a pattern over time, but police cannot begin to recognize it as a pattern unless victims report the crimes. Even if the victim waited several years to report, if the offender has continued to commit crimes, the victim's evidence may still be used in a criminal case to establish a pattern, or for sentencing information, in another current case.

CONTACTING THE POLICE

Once you call the police, do not reenter or move about in the areas where the offender was present. These areas will become the *crime scene* and may produce evidence to convict the offender of the crime. If you have been physically injured, or there is or other bodily fluids on (or in) you, resist the urge to wash up. Do not change your clothes. The hospital will want to collect these items as evidence. And if you use a towel or other item to wipe the blood off, tell the police, so that it can be collected.

THE ROLE OF HOSPITALS AND MEDICAL PERSONNEL

If the victim does not report the crime to police, but instead seeks treatment at a hospital or medical facility, in certain states the hospital is required by state law to notify the police if treating a crime victim. The victim may choose to proceed with charges or not, but the police will come to the hospital.

Hospitals are a part of the criminal justice system because they can be a collector of evidence on the victim's body. For example, in a rape case, the hospital can collect hairs, fibers, semen, saliva, and blood left by the offender on the victim. In most states, this examination is free of charge, and some states have a standardized evidence collection kit. If the victim presses charges, the hospital gives the evidence directly to police.

Do not be afraid to ask medical personnel what the procedures and tests are that you are going through. Some hospitals have a crisis or social worker who can come to the emergency room to explain procedures. Others may call a crisis worker upon your request. You may not be able to understand everything, but it may help calm you to know what is happening.

If you have blood on your clothes, or other evidence of the crime, your clothes will be taken as evidence. In such a case, you will need a change of clothes. Sometimes, hospitals have sweatsuits or other clothing to give to the victim. If you are a family member or loved one, be sure to bring clothing for the victim. It can often help to regain a sense of control to have your own clothing after the emergency medical treatment.

THE POLICE INVESTIGATION 6

Police are responsible for taking crime reports, investigating, collecting evidence, and apprehending suspects. Investigation includes questioning the victim and all witnesses to the crime, and identifying, collecting, and analyzing evidence to prove the existence of the crime. Any item of information that can be used to prove an element of the crime is considered evidence.

Upon arrival on the scene, the responding officer should begin by identifying him or herself and determining what crime occurred. Police officers are now trained in *crisis intervention* techniques that are designed to increase their sensitivity to the stress of the victim. The officer will immediately determine whether emergency medical treatment is necessary and call for the appropriate assistance.

THE VICTIM INTERVIEW

The officer will question the victim to obtain preliminary information. The victim will be asked to described what happened (date, time, place, details) and to provide information concerning the defendant's identity or description. For example, the officer will want to know how the offender made contact with you. The offender may be following a pattern; he may be an experienced criminal who commits crimes only at certain times or in certain places.

Sometimes, the offender will "test" the victim before a robbery, mugging, or other attack. This testing can be a brief period of conversation, like asking for help or directions. It is important, if possible, for you to recall the exact words that were used. What actions did the offender engage in? The offender may have a telltale nervous habit such as a twitch or muscle tic that can help identify him or her. During the attack, it is important to remember what the offender did, said, and touched.

Finally, did the offender threaten you by telling you not to call the police, or warn you that he knew where you lived or worked? Sometimes, an offender will boast about other crimes he has committed.

Example: During a robbery, the robber might say, "don't be like that other man and fight me now." Police can use that information to try to link the offender with other area crimes with similar patterns.

Police recognize that the shock of the crime may cause a victim's initial statement to be confused or disorganized. If the officer asks clarifying questions, do not assume that the officer is challenging you or does not believe you. He or she simply may need more details. You may not know the answer to some of the questions or remember certain details. If you do not know or cannot remember, let the officer know that. Do not try to fill in the gaps with what you think or guess. At a follow-up interview you may remember more.

Police also are trained to understand that many victims may express their frustration and fears through anger, and may direct some of their anger at the officer. They do not usually take it personally.

After the responding officer has obtained preliminary information, the suspect's description will be broadcast to other officers in the area and a search for the offender will begin. The responding officer will continue to question any other witnesses to the crime.

THE CRIME SCENE

The *crime scene* is a phrase used to describe any area of the crime in which evidence might be present that helps prove the crime. A crime scene can be a car, bedroom, house, business, section of woods, trail, or any other place where the crime occurred. Police will immediately close off the crime scene so that no one except evidence technicians have access, until all potential physical evidence is collected. If the crime scene is outside, it is very important that police immediately close the area to traffic so it does not become contaminated by people moving through it.

The crime scene may contain physical evidence such as fibers, hair, stains, fingerprints, or footprints. The victim can help police identify the crime scene area by pointing out how and where the offender came into contact with the victim, the movement of the offender, and what was touched during the crime. The victim can also identify what the offender took from the crime scene upon leaving. As noted above, even the victim can be part of the crime scene if the attack was a personal assault.

Police will collect all items that may contain evidence and mark it for review by crime lab scientists. Crime laboratories exist in all states. The Federal Bureau of Investigation (FBI) also does crime analysis. The laboratory receives the evidence and scientifically analyzes it to determine what it is and where it may have come from.

Example: In a case where the victim is murdered, fibers removed from the victim's body may be identified as matching the carpet of a certain make and model of car. This evidence is then reported to the investigator on the case who may be able to link that type of car with the defendant.

THE DETECTIVE'S ROLE

If the offender is known, the police will attempt to locate and question that person. If the victim or witnesses do not know the identity of the offender, and the suspect is not immediately found from the description given, a report is completed and the case is usually turned over to a detective or investigator for follow-up.

The detective or investigator continues the investigation into the facts of the crime. This officer is usually more experienced than the patrol or responding officer, and will follow up all leads in an effort to identify and collect evidence. The detective will likely need to re-interview the victim. This time the interview will be in much greater detail in an effort to uncover additional information that might help in the investigation. If the suspect is unknown, the detective may investigate possible candidates for motives and alibis.

THE RIGHTS OF THE VICTIM

Under victim's rights laws, the victim has a right in many states to request information on the status of the investigation, and where it does not compromise the investigation, the police will usually provide that information. Although it is the practice of many police officers to routinely keep the victim informed, it is a good idea to write a letter to the detective or investigator requesting to be kept informed of the status of the investigation. (see Chapter 3 and form A in Appendix D.)

Address the request to the police officer in charge of the investigation, usually called an investigator or detective. Usually this is the officer who will maintain contact with you to provide updates and information as the case progresses, but sometimes a victim must contact the police station to find out who has been assigned to the case. Once the name of the investigator is available, do not be afraid to call that person and ask about the case. This keeps the case on the mind of an investigator who may have several ongoing cases. After the interviews, periodically ask to meet with the investigator to talk about the case.

Because you will have a lot of unfamiliar feelings and questions, it might help if you keep a log and write down your questions and the names of the persons you have spoken to in the police department concerning your case. Also, if you remember additional details, you should write these down and contact the police promptly with this information. You may be unaware that you possess vital information, or you may remember something that the police do not know.

ARRESTING THE OFFENDER 7

IDENTIFYING THE OFFENDER

The police have a variety of methods to track down the identity of possible suspects. If the suspect is caught near the scene shortly after the crime, and the victim is able, the victim may be asked to identify the offender in a procedure called a *showup*. In a showup, the suspect is shown to the victim for identification purposes. A showup may be on-scene, or at the police station, or the victim may be taken to the suspect by police car.

A victim may also go to the police station to look through a series of *mug book* pictures of prior offenders or to help an artist make a composite drawing in an effort to identify the suspect. Or the victim may go to the police station to attend a *lineup* procedure.

LINEUP PROCEDURES

Lineups can be in-person or by photos. Many victims fear in-person lineups because they think the offender can see them. In an in-person lineup, several persons matching the same general description are literally lined up with the suspect. The victim views the suspects through a one-way mirror or with some other device that permits the victim to see the individuals, while they cannot see the victim. If the suspect has been charged with a crime, he or she has a right to have an attorney present. The suspect's attorney will be permitted to observe you as you examine the lineup participants.

The police detective should first explain the procedures involved in the lineup, and keep you out of sight of the offender. Do not hesitate to ask the officer to stay near you during the identification procedure, if you feel concerned. The officer will ask you if you recognize any of the individuals, and, if so, how you know them. Take your time in looking at the lineup, and if you can identify the offender, do so clearly. This establishes the identification of the defendant as the offender without any prompting from the police.

In smaller jurisdictions where an in-person lineup is not feasible, a photo lineup may be used. Several photos are shown to the victim depicting similar looking individuals. The victim is then asked the same questions as in the in-person lineup procedure.

UNKNOWN OFFENDERS

If the victim does not know the identity of the offender and cannot spot him through the mug books, the police may use new scientific advances in an effort to identify the attacker. For example, DNA (deoxyribonucleic acid) is the new "fingerprint" evidence. DNA identifies a person by his or her genes because every person's DNA is unique. If the offender leaves his or her DNA at the scene through blood, saliva, or semen, the police can collect it and send it to a crime lab for identification.

MAKING THE ARREST

Once sufficient information is available, if the offender can be found, police should arrest the suspect. Upon arrest, the defendant will be read his *Miranda* rights to remain silent and to obtain an attorney. If the defendant chooses not to talk to police, they cannot continue to question him. If the defendant chooses to talk, any statement the defendant gives to police will be closely scrutinized later to determine whether the defendant's rights were violated and whether the statement was given voluntarily.

After the arrest, police continue to gather evidence to meet the legal elements of the case.

Example: Upon arrest, the offender's clothes and body are examined for possible evidence. The police will take his or her clothes as potential evidence. Photographs of the offender may be taken to show any identifying marks or defensive wounds the victim may have inflicted.

The police will continue to search for any property taken from the victim. For example, if the charge is based on a home invasion in which several items are stolen, the police will search for and try to recover any of the stolen property to be used as evidence in the case. All persons have a right against unreasonable search and seizure, and the police may be required to obtain search warrants from a judge in order to collect some of the evidence.

WHAT IF POLICE DO NOT MAKE AN ARREST?

In any number of cases, police may not arrest a suspect. There may be insufficient evidence of all the legally required elements of the crime, or the offender may never be identified. If police do have sufficient evidence, the offender may have fled the jurisdiction or gone into hiding to evade arrest. If the police do not make an arrest once the suspect is known or his whereabouts are known, the victim can request that the police continue the investigation as new information is uncovered. The victim should also ask to meet with the investigator to find out why an arrest has not been made. If the victim is not able to meet with the investigator, ask to meet with the Chief of Detectives, a Captain, or even the Chief of Police for an explanation. If the police will not arrest the suspect, the victim can go to the local prosecutor's office or the Attorney General's office and seek assistance.

FILING THE CHARGE 8

MAKING THE DECISION TO FILE

Because the government must prosecute a criminal case, the final decision to pursue a state charge rests with a county or city prosecutor (also known by other names such as a district attorney, parish prosecutor, borough prosecutor, or state attorney). For federal charges the decision rests with the U.S. Attorney's Office. For felony cases, once police have completed their investigation, the file and all reports are provided to the prosecutor's office for consideration. In some jurisdictions for misdemeanor cases, police may recommend that charges be filed, or may file a charge if a police officer witnessed the offense. Similarly, the victim may also pursue a misdemeanor charge against a defendant by appearing before a court officer and requesting a charge be filed. In all cases, the prosecutor represents the government.

SCREENING THE CASE

Prosecutors have a great deal of discretion in deciding what to charge, and the law may permit the prosecutor to choose from several different possible charges. For example, a prosecutor may choose to file a less serious misdemeanor rather than a felony in a given case. The prosecutor may also choose not to file a charge at all, usually based on one or more of the following reasons:

- reasonable doubt of the suspect's guilt;

- reluctance of a key witness to testify;

- cooperation of the accused in the arrest of others;

- a legal element of the case is not present; or

- the circumstances of the crime are such that a jury is unlikely to convict.

If a decision is made not to prosecute, some larger prosecutor's offices have established a review process, sometimes called *felony review*. If you believe the prosecutor did not have all the evidence or failed to consider a crucial piece of information, a review should be requested and the prosecutor should reconsider filing charges in light of the additional evidence. If the prosecutor still refuses to charge, consider contacting the head of the prosecutor's office or your state's attorney general for assistance.

METHODS OF CHARGING

There are generally three methods by which a crime can be charged: *complaint*, *information*, and *indictment*. In some jurisdictions, petty offenses and less serious misdemeanors are charged by a complaint form. This complaint may be made by the victim or the prosecutor on a form provided by the county or municipal criminal court clerk's office.

For felony crimes, the prosecutor signs the complaint, which may be called an information. The case then goes before a judge at a preliminary hearing to determine whether there is sufficient evidence to proceed with bringing the defendant to trial. The prosecutor can also take the case before a grand jury to seek an indictment. In some states, even if the grand jury refuses to indict, the prosecutor can still file a complaint.

THE GRAND JURY

The *grand jury* process may be used instead of the preliminary hearing (see Chapter 9 for an explanation of preliminary hearings) or in addition to a preliminary hearing. A grand jury is like any other jury. It is made up of citizens usually selected from the voter or motor vehicle registration lists. The grand jury determines whether charges should proceed in criminal cases brought before it.

The prosecutor presents evidence to the grand jury who will determine whether there is probable cause to charge the defendant. If the grand jury believes there is probable cause, they render a *true bill*. If not, they render *no bill*. (Generally, the grand jury will render a true bill because only the prosecutor presents evidence at the grand jury hearing. Therefore, the grand jury usually does not hear any evidence that tends to indicate the defendant is not guilty.) If a true bill is returned, the defendant is indicted and a warrant will be issued for his or her arrest. If no bill is returned, the case does not go forward. If the defendant has already been picked up, he or she is released.

TIME LIMITS

With the exception of murder, nearly all offenses have time limits within which the charges must be filed against the suspect. There are exceptions to the time limits, and each state varies in the limitation period it permits for charging crimes. These time limits are called *statutes of limitation*, since they literally limit the time within which a charge can be brought. Even if the offense has a time limit, there are exceptions to the statutes of limitation.

Example: If the suspect flees the jurisdiction before he or she can be arrested, the time period stops while the suspect is absent from the state.

SPECIAL CASES   Many states have also extended the time period for cases in which the victim is a child and for some types of sex offenses. These crimes cause serious trauma that may keep a victim from reporting the crime to authorities for a long period of time. It may be only after the victim becomes an adult that the crime can be safely reported to police. A number of states have extended the time limit for charging this kind of case.

THE CHARGES IN YOUR CASE

To fully understand what crimes are charged in your case, obtain the exact statutory citation, which will be listed on the charges filed against the defendant. Ask your prosecutor or victim-witness coordinator to provide you with a copy of the charges. With these statutory section numbers, you can find the state's criminal code, which will list the elements and the potential sentences for each crime. (See Appendix B on legal research.)

Pretrial Procedures 9

The procedures before trial often determine the strength of the prosecution and defense case, and will narrow the issues to be raised at the trial. This is the longest part of the criminal case and can take more than a year to complete. Critics of the criminal justice system have argued that it is very painful for the victim to keep waiting for a resolution of their case, and in some jurisdictions there have been efforts to speed up the process. Nevertheless, the defendant often benefits by extending the time, hoping the victim will give up or maybe just move away and leave no forwarding address.

The Role of the Judge

A judge presides over the criminal case. Today, most judges are attorneys with experience in criminal trials. When a legal question arises, the judge makes the decision based on the laws, procedures, and previous case decisions. He or she has a duty to remain impartial and to see that the criminal justice process is fair and just for all participants. This means that the judge should not take sides.

If a *jury* has been requested, the judge oversees the selection of a jury to be sure that a jury of the defendant's peers is chosen. The judge will determine whether the state has enough evidence to proceed with trial, and is also the person who approves continuances. Once a jury is chosen, the judge will determine what evidence can be heard, subject to the applicable criminal law and rules of procedure. If a jury has not been requested, the trial is called a *bench trial* and the judge will decide both questions of law and fact.

All states have rules of evidence and procedure that govern the prosecutor and defense questioning of the victim and other witnesses. If one side objects to a question, it is the judge who will decide whether the witness must answer the question.

THE VICTIM'S RIGHTS

In most states, the victim has the right to know what the status of the case is prior to trial. In some states, prosecutors will automatically notify the victims of pending dates, but it is also common that the victim must request information. If your state requires that you request this information, be sure to put your request in writing. For a sample letter to the prosecutor, see form B in Appendix D.

In many states, the victim's rights laws permit the victim to be present at court proceedings, subject to the rules of evidence, on the same basis as the defendant, or at the judge's discretion. The rules of evidence govern whether a witness can be present in court. For example, courts often allow a prosecutor or defense motion to exclude witnesses where one witness' testimony might be improperly influenced by watching another witness testify.

If the defense tries to have you excluded from the proceedings, make an oral or written request to the prosecutor to permit you to stay in the courtroom. Unless the defense can show a valid reason why you should be kept out, you should be able to stay.

Also, some states permit you to have a support person present in court. The same objection should be made if the defense tries to keep out that person. The judge will make the final decision on whether you can be present and under what circumstances.

Victims are entitled to be free from intimidation and harassment while attending court proceedings. A secure or safe waiting area may mean a separate waiting room, or waiting in the office of the prosecutor or the victim-witness coordinator, or it may mean waiting in an empty jury room or office. If no provisions have been made in advance, ask the prosecutor for assistance in directing you to a waiting area that minimizes your contact with the defendant, his family, and his friends while awaiting hearings. If you or your family are harassed, threatened, or harmed at any time during the criminal proceedings, immediately notify police and the prosecutor so that appropriate action can be taken to protect you or your family.

THE RIGHT TO A SPEEDY TRIAL

The defendant has a right to a speedy trial, which is defined by law. The time period is shorter if the defendant remains in jail pending trial. The defendant can demand that the state meet the time limits and if it fails, the case will be dismissed and the defendant is released. If the state violates the defendant's speedy trial rights, the defendant cannot be retried because it would violate the U.S. Constitution. However, in many cases the defendant requests a continuance, and is required to waive his right to a speedy trial, at least for the period of delay he seeks.

Some states have provided that the victim has a right to a *speedy disposition*. This right is not accorded the same weight as the defendant's rights, but it may entitle the victim to object to delay, or the prosecutor to raise the effect of continuances on victims. Some judges are becoming more sensitive to the needs of victims in determining whether to grant continuances. Violation of victim's right to a speedy disposition will not result in dismissal or release of the defendant.

ARRAIGNMENT —
DEFENDANT'S INITIAL APPEARANCE

Within a short time after arrest, the accused, now called the defendant, is brought before a judge for the initial appearance, called an *arraignment*. The arraignment proceeding informs the defendant of the charges and provides an opportunity for the defendant to make a *plea* of guilty, not guilty, or no contest.

If the defendant pleads *guilty*, he admits the charges and a conviction can be entered against him. A *not guilty* plea means that the case will continue towards trial. In a *no contest*, or *nolo contendere* plea, the defendant does not admit anything and agrees that the court may enter a conviction against him (nolo contendere means "I will not contest"). A no contest plea is helpful for the defendant because the facts of the case are not proven and thus cannot be used in a later civil trial as evidence of guilt. If the defendant does not answer or make a plea, it will be presumed that the plea is not guilty.

At this first hearing, an attorney will be appointed for the defendant if he cannot afford private counsel. The defendant has a right to have the charges read, but many defendant's waive this right. The defendant will likely plead not guilty. Where bail has not been preset, the judge makes the decision to grant or deny bail to the defendant. The date for the next hearing, usually called a *preliminary hearing*, will most likely be scheduled at this time.

BAIL

Most defendants are eligible for release pending trial. *Bail* is the method by which a defendant provides money or other security to insure his return to court. The *bond* is the document that the defendant signs, which identifies what was posted (e.g., money, house, etc.) as his security. In the least serious cases, pretrial release is permitted without bail, and bail is generally available to most defendants who are charged with a crime. Exceptions differ by state law, but generally certain types of murder charges are nonbailable offenses. Originally, the purpose of bail was to ensure that the defendant would return to court for the trial, and the amount set was high enough to secure the defendant's return while not being excessive, which would violate his or her constitutional rights. Today, in addition to securing the defendant's appearance for trial, the protection of the public is also a consideration in setting bail.

THE BAIL
HEARING
The amount of bail is preset for some crimes, so the defendant will know exactly how much he or she has to produce to gain release. If the defendant can produce bail, he or she can be released within a short time after the arrest. Many victims are shocked to see the defendant out on the street the day after being arrested.

In serious felonies, bail is not usually preset, and a bail hearing will be held to determine the amount and conditions of bail. In a bail hearing, the court will consider:

- the nature and circumstances of the crime, including whether there was force, weapons, impact on, and injuries to, the victim;

- the likelihood that the prosecution may upgrade the charge to a more serious offense;

- the defendant's attempts, if any, to avoid prosecution;

- the defendant's ties to the community;

- the defendant's prior criminal history;

- the potential sentence for the offense charged; and

- relevant victim information.

Today, the prosecutor can present evidence of the defendant's dangerousness, and the judge will consider whether the defendant is a threat to the victim, the victim's family, or the public in deciding whether to grant bail. In California, for example, the protection of the public is a primary concern in bail consideration.

Generalized fear of the defendant will not usually be sufficient, but the presence of threats by the defendant during the crime, or the actions of the defendant's family or friends in intimidating the victim should be brought to the prosecutor's attention prior to any hearing on bail so that the judge can take that into consideration when determining whether to grant bail. If the defendant has made threats against you or you have reason to fear that the defendant knows where you work or live, ask your prosecutor to request the judge to deny bail to the defendant.

If the defendant is granted bail, he or she must usually put up a bond. In rare cases the *bond* is the defendant's word that he will return. The defendant who is permitted to sign for his release is said to be released on his *recognizance*.

More likely, the defendant will have to post a monetary bond. The exact amount of the bond depends on state law, but it may be some percentage of the total amount, and it can be deposited in money, property, or other item of value. Some jurisdictions permit a defendant to post a percentage of the court-ordered bail amount. The court is entitled to an administration fee and will return the deposit if the defendant meets the conditions of bond. If the defendant does not, the full court-ordered amount is forfeited.

Bail is usually higher in felonies because of the seriousness of the crime. If the defendant, cannot deposit the amount required, or if bail is denied, the defendant will remain in jail while awaiting trial.

CONDITIONS OF BAIL

If the defendant is out on bail pending trial, every state has certain conditions that must be met, and additional conditions that can be required by the judge for the defendant to remain free. Mandatory conditions commonly include that the defendant:

- appear at all court dates;
- follow all court orders;

- remain in the state pending trial; and

- commit no crimes pending trial.

If the prosecutor produces evidence that other conditions are necessary to protect the victim, victim's family, or the public before trial, the court can include other items, such as that the defendant:

- possess no firearms;

- refrain from communicating to the victim or the victim's family;

- refrain from following the victim or appearing at the victim's school or work;

- refrain from alcohol or drug use;

- undergo alcohol or drug treatment;

- undergo counseling;

- get or keep a job;

- attend school;

- support his or her dependents;

- observe a curfew;

- remain in the custody of another person or agency;

- be supervised by another person or agency; and

- vacate the household (if the victim is a family member).

In Utah, the victim has a right to appear before the judge to provide input on issues related to the defendant's release. In most states, however, the prosecutor is charged with presenting evidence on dangerousness, so make sure to tell the prosecutor before the hearing to include as a condition of bail that the defendant stay away from your work, home, and family.

Get a copy of the court order listing the conditions of defendant's pretrial release. If you believe the defendant has violated any of the conditions, tell the prosecutor right away. Call the police if the violation is immediate, so you can get help and the violation can be recorded. When the defendant violates conditions of pretrial release, he or she can lose the right to freedom while awaiting trial.

PRELIMINARY HEARING

This hearing is usually held soon after the defendant's initial court appearance. The purpose of this hearing is to determine whether probable cause exists that a crime was committed, and that this defendant committed the crime. This hearing will be held before the judge. The police officer will testify and the victim may also be called as a witness.

The defendant does not have to produce any witnesses (remember he has no burden of proving his case), but does have the right to cross-examine any prosecution witness at this hearing. After the witnesses have been presented, the judge will either determine that there is sufficient evidence to continue to trial, or dismiss the case and release the defendant.

PRE-TRIAL MOTIONS

Most criminal court cases are delayed for a considerable time period while the state and defendant investigate the case. Both the state and the defendant may request information and may file *motions* to discover information. Motions are merely oral or written requests made to a judge. Motions can involve the charges, witnesses, or evidence. Many motions will not require the victim's presence, such as motions directed at the legal validity of the charges or motions to admit other crimes evidence. Even so, in some states, notice of scheduled hearings on these motions may be provided to victims. Some common motions include:

MOTION TO DISMISS | A motion to dismiss can be made by the state or defendant. Sometimes the state will elect to proceed on a few of many possible charges, and so may dismiss the rest at some point prior to trial. The defendant may also ask the court to dismiss the case on the basis that the charge is defective because it fails to meet the legal requirements. A defendant may also ask the court to dismiss the case when the state failed to meet his or her speedy trial rights.

MOTION TO
SUPPRESS

The defendant may make a motion to suppress the introduction of evidence of his arrest or his identification by the victim. This motion is also made by the defendant to stop the state from using a confession or other evidence obtained in violation of the defendant's rights. For example, the defendant may argue that the confession was not voluntary, or he or she was denied the right to legal counsel, or that items were taken from him or her in an unreasonable search or seizure. If such a motion is granted by the judge, the state would not be able to use that confession or item of evidence against the defendant at trial. Hopefully, the other evidence against the defendant will be sufficient for a conviction.

MOTION FOR
CONTINUANCE

Trials may be continued for legitimate reasons, like a delay in analyzing evidence or witness unavailability, but many cases are continued at the request of the defendant as a strategy to make the victim drop out of the case. Judges are trained to scrutinize the reasons for continuance requests. In some states special consideration must be given to the effect of a continuance on the victim.

Example: In Ohio, the victim can object to a substantial delay in proceedings, and upon request, the prosecutor will file a motion with the court to consider the victim's wishes.

MOTION FOR
CHANGE OF
JUDGE OR VENUE

If the judge is prejudiced or if, for example, pretrial publicity is so biased that the defendant cannot get a fair trial, these motions may be filed seeking to change the judge or move the trial.

MOTIONS FOR
DISCOVERY

These very common motions are often searches for evidence. Most motions relate to the identification, analysis, or production of forensic or scientific evidence. Some motions may involve questions surrounding identification and qualification of expert witnesses.

With regard to discovering information concerning the victim, states apply differing approaches. Victims may generally refuse to speak to, or to be interviewed by, the defendant or defense investigators. In some states, however, the victim may be required or ordered to attend a deposition to give a statement before a court reporter under oath. In others, depositions are not permitted in criminal court. To protect its victims, an Arizona constitutional amendment provides that victims may refuse interviews, depositions, or other discovery requests.

PLEA BARGAINING 10

Plea bargaining has existed in some form in the United States since the early 1800s. Today, it is not unusual for some jurisdictions to resolve 80-90% of their felony cases by plea bargain. It is called a bargain because both the state and the defendant derive some benefit by the deal. The state does not have to risk a trial and the possibility of losing (and the defendant gets at least some punishment and a criminal record); the defendant does not have to risk a longer or more severe sentence. The judge must still approve of the agreement before it can be entered in the court. A judge can also reject a plea bargain.

TYPES OF PLEA BARGAINS

There are two major types of plea bargains. In the first type, the defendant negotiates away certain charges so that only a lesser charge (or charges) remain pending.

Example: If a defendant is facing two charges—a home invasion with a possible sentence of 6-30 years and burglary with a possible sentence of 3-7 years—by pleading guilty to the burglary in exchange for dismissing the home invasion, the defendant has reduced his potential sentence to a maximum of 7 years (instead of 30).

The second type involves an agreement by the state and defendant to a particular sentence in exchange for a guilty plea. In the above example, the state and defendant would agree that the prosecutor would ask for no more than 15 years on the home invasion (rather than the 30 possible), and 3 years on the burglary (rather than 7).

PROCEDURES

Plea negotiations most often take place very early in a case. In this way, the defendant "tests" the confidence of the prosecutor to see how strong the state thinks its case is, or the state may "test" the defendant to see how readily the case can be disposed. For example, if the prosecutor feels the evidence is weak or a victim is wavering, the state may readily agree to a plea bargain.

Similarly, if the defendant is not confident of his ability to win at trial, but can arrange a lesser sentence or a reduced charge, the defendant may be willing to plead guilty. The earlier the offer, the more likely it will be generous, but a plea bargain may be reached at any time, even in the middle of the trial.

The defendant has certain constitutional rights in making a plea, and his plea must be voluntary. Therefore, even if the judge approves of the agreement, there will be a short hearing before a court reporter in which the defendant will be questioned as to his understanding of the plea.

THE VICTIM'S ROLE

Because of the critical impact that a plea bargain has on the victim, states now permit or require prosecutors to confer or consult with victims before an agreement is made. Some states require prosecutors to consider the victim's concerns prior to engaging in plea negotiations (these are currently Arizona, Illinois, Kentucky, Montana, New Hampshire, Ohio, Pennsylvania, South Carolina, South Dakota, and West Virginia). At least one state (Maine) requires the prosecutor to state the victim's wishes in court before an agreement is approved by a judge.

To include victim impact information, some states require the victim to prepare a victim impact statement. See the section in Chapter 13 on " The Victim Impact Statement" for details on what should be included in such a statement.

THE CRIMINAL TRIAL 11

If the defendant does not plead guilty, the case will go to trial. The United States Constitution (which is the Federal Constitution) requires the government to follow certain rules before a person can be convicted of a crime, and this has led to the passage of many laws protecting a defendant's rights. The prosecution of a criminal case is by an *adversary* process, which means that both sides can present evidence to prove the guilt or innocence of the defendant.

DEFENDANT'S RIGHT TO A JURY

The trial may be by jury in serious criminal cases. Sometimes, it is the defendant's strategy to demand a jury, because in most states, the verdict of the jury must be unanimous to convict. If the defendant can convince even one juror not to vote for conviction, then no guilty verdict will be entered against him or her. In some cases, the defendant may choose to waive a jury trial, and the case is tried by the judge and is called a *bench* trial.

Each state has adopted procedures for jury selection. Random pools of jurors are picked to appear and answer the questions of a judge or the attorneys in a questioning process called *voir dire* (pronounced "vwa dear"). The questions determine whether a proposed juror is qualified to serve on a particular jury and to identify grounds for removal. Once a jury has been selected, the trial is ready to begin.

OPENING STATEMENT

The trial begins with an overview of the case, called an *opening statement*, given by each party or their attorney. The state has the entire burden of proving the case, so it goes first. The prosecutor outlines the theory of the case and what he or she believes the witnesses and any other evidence will prove to the jury (or to the judge in a bench trial).

The defense also has the right to make an opening statement, which will sometimes be given right after the prosecutor's opening statement, and sometimes be given just before the defense attorney begins presenting his or her evidence. The defense attorney may wish to delay his or her opening statement until the prosecution has finished presenting all of its evidence. This is because it may be difficult for the defense attorney to decide what witnesses he will call until he has heard and seen the prosecution's evidence.

If the prosecution has not presented a good case, the defense attorney may decide that he does not need to present any testimony (since the prosecutor has the burden of proof, and the defendant is innocent until proven guilty beyond a reasonable doubt and cannot be required to testify).

EVIDENCE AND TESTIMONY

All of the information that can be considered by a judge or jury in a criminal trial is presented through witness testimony and by introducing documents, physical items, and scientific evidence. Each state has rules that govern the admissibility of evidence, and not all information that is relevant will be permitted to be introduced into the trial. For example, information that is highly prejudicial to the defendant, like a long-past criminal conviction, is weighed against its importance to the current case before it can be admitted.

One notable exception is California, which constitutionally provides for "truth in evidence" in criminal trials. California's Constitution provides that "relevant evidence shall not be excluded" in juvenile or criminal offenses except under specified circumstances. (CA Const. Article (Art.) I, Sec. 28(d).)

Most of the preliminary motions have determined what evidence will be permitted at trial, but some questions may arise during trial. Objections may be raised by either the state or defendant for many reasons. The judge must then decide the matter before the trial continues.

Each side will present witnesses by direct examination. The questions will be asked first by the attorney who is sponsoring the witness, followed by cross-examination by the opposing attorney.

Example: A prosecution witness might be the police officer. The prosecutor asks questions on direct examination of the officer, which is followed by cross-examination by the defense.

DIRECT EXAMINATION

The purpose of direct examination is to tell the story, to find out what happened, so the questions will be open-ended and allow the witness to explain the event. An example follows:

Prosecutor:	"State your name and occupation."
Police Officer:	"John Doe. I am a police officer with the Gotham City Police Department."
Prosecutor:	"Do you recall the night of January 1, 1996?"
Police Officer:	"Yes."
Prosecutor:	"Tell the court what happened on that night."
Police Officer:	"I was on duty that night, and at approximately 12:10 a.m., while driving my patrol car at the corner of Elm and Fifth Street, I observed a woman on the curb waving her arm at me."

CROSS
EXAMINATION

The purpose of cross-examination is to limit or test the witness' recollection of the event, or to show that the witness has not told the entire story or is lying, in an attempt to undermine their credibility and reduce the impact of their testimony in the case. Cross-examination can also be used to show the bias, interest, or motive of the witness. The questions are designed to lead the witness to a particular answer.

Police are often attacked in a criminal case by the defense as a strategy to undermine the evidence against the defendant. The defense attorney in the example above has checked the police roster for January 2nd, and found that the police officer was not on duty that day. He also noticed that the date on the officer's police report is January 6th. This led to the following exchange on cross examination:

Defense Attorney:	"Isn't it a fact you were *not* on duty that night?"
Police Officer:	"No. I was on duty until 11:55 p.m., and was on my way home in my patrol car when I first saw Ms. Smith."
Defense Attorney:	"Isn't it true that you didn't even complete your police report until several days later?"
Police Officer:	"Yes. I didn't complete my report until I could speak with a particular witness again."
Defense Attorney:	"So you don't really remember that night, do you?"
Police Officer:	"I remember that night very clearly."

Here, the defense attorney's attempt to discredit the officer was not very successful, but you should get the idea of the difference between the tone of direct examination and cross-examination.

THE STATE'S CASE

Because the state goes first, it chooses the order in which the state's witnesses will testify. Depending on the type of case, and an evaluation of available evidence, the prosecutor may have the victim testify first, but may also call other witnesses to "set the stage" for the victim's later testimony. Typical witnesses include police officers who investigated the case, evidence and lab technicians who collected and analyzed the evidence, eyewitnesses, and experts who can assist the judge or jury in understanding the evidence to be presented.

THE VICTIM AS A WITNESS

PREPARATION FOR COURT

The victim may be the state's primary witness in the case and will usually be required to testify at trial. You have likely waited a long time for this day. Now that it has come, you are likely to be nervous and maybe frightened. You may have experienced testifying at the preliminary hearing or at some other pretrial motion, but that was some time ago.

The emotions experienced during the crime can be rekindled at the court hearings. For example, anger, fear, and hatred may interfere with your ability to tell the story. Today, you will be confronting the offender in court. The defendant's family and friends may also be in the courtroom watching you. The best way to overcome these fears is to be prepared.

Preparation by the prosecutor will help you, but you should also make an attempt to familiarize yourself with court procedures. If possible, make a visit to other courtrooms to watch testimony in unrelated cases. Sometimes victim-witness personnel in the prosecutor's office can set up a time to tour the courtroom in which you will likely testify. Even televised courtroom documentary programs may help you visualize the court process. Watch carefully the demeanor of the witnesses who testify and especially become aware of the role of the defense attorney and of the strategies used in defending cases.

TESTIFYING IN COURT

A victim's demeanor in testifying is very important. Sometimes, in an effort to be calm and controlled, the jury may think the victim is too unemotional to be genuine. But if the victim is too relaxed, the defense attorney may use that fact against him or her.

In preparing you to testify, the prosecutor will likely suggest that you:

- tell the truth;

- do not volunteer information;

- do not use drugs or alcohol to calm nerves;

- do not memorize testimony;

- be straightforward and speak clearly;

- say so, if you are unsure of the question;

- look at the judge or jury when answering a question;

- listen carefully to each question before answering;

- dress conservatively;

- understand that the goal of the defense attorney is to discredit you;

- if a question cannot be answered with a yes or no, say so, or explain that you must give two answers to the two-part question;

- do not guess at answering. If you do not know the answer, say "I don't know;"

- if you are interrupted before you finish your answer, ask if you can finish your first answer to the first question before answering a new question;

- objections: both the prosecutor and defense attorney will object. If so, stop talking and wait for the judge to rule;

- do not follow the commands or instructions of the defense attorney; only the judge can issue orders;

- do not argue with the defense attorney; and

- control your anger.

If it seems like that is a lot to remember—it is. But, just do your best. You know what happened, so tell it as best you can to the judge and jury. You are not in control of all the rules and procedures, but you are in control of yourself.

THE DEFENSE CASE

After the state completes its case, the defendant is entitled to introduce his evidence throughout the same methods. The defendant may introduce *alibi* witnesses or witnesses who attack the evidence offered by the state. In criminal cases, however, the defendant has a constitutional right not to testify and the state may not suggest any reason for the defendant's failure to testify. The state has the same right as the defendant to cross-examine the defense witnesses.

CLOSING STATEMENT

After each side has completed its case, the state and defendant summarize their cases through closing arguments. The state will argue that the case has been proved beyond a reasonable doubt and will likely remind the judge or jury of each important witness' testimony. The defendant will argue that the state failed to prove that the defendant committed the crime beyond a reasonable doubt.

The defendant may also attack the state's witnesses as being unreliable or having a motive to lie, and therefore suggest that the evidence was false or improperly used against him. Once the defendant completes closing argument, the state will usually have one more chance to convince the judge or jury that the evidence was sufficient to convict the defendant.

THE VERDICT 12

THE ROLE OF THE JURY

Once both sides have completed their presentation of evidence and testimony, the case moves to deliberation on a verdict. There are a range of possible verdicts in most states, including guilty, guilty but mentally ill, not guilty, and not guilty by reason of insanity. Contrary to what you may hear from members of the news media, *innocent* is not available as either a plea or a verdict.

In freeing a defendant, all a jury determines is that the state did not prove guilt; not that the defendant proved innocence. The *guilty* verdicts permit the entry of a judgment of conviction and permit a sentence to be imposed on the defendant. The *not guilty* verdicts do not permit either conviction or a sentence.

INSANITY   *Not guilty by reason of insanity* developed from the concept that the law should not hold a person criminally accountable for actions over which he has no control. If a person lacks the ability to control his actions due to mental illness, then he is not to be blamed and should not be punished for his actions.

States differ on the standards and degrees to which the defense of insanity will be permitted. A person found not guilty by reason of insanity is usually released (unless someone begins a civil court proceeding to have him committed to a mental institution as being a danger to himself or others).

MENTAL ILLNESS

Because of public outrage over some defendants' attempts to use an insanity defense (and thereby get released), some states have adopted a verdict of *guilty but mentally ill*. If the jurors believe that the defendant did commit the illegal act, but has a mental illness, they may render a verdict of guilty but mentally ill. This verdict keeps the defendant in custody, and merely influences where he serves his sentence.

Upon conviction, the defendant undergoes a psychiatric evaluation to determine the nature and extent of his mental illness, then the defendant is sent to a mental health facility to serve his sentence and receive treatment. If the defendant regains his mental health during the period of his sentence, he is transferred to prison for the remainder of the term.

INSTRUCTIONS

In a *jury trial*, the judge instructs the jury on the law to be applied in its deliberation, and then the case goes to the jury. The jury's job is to determine whether the facts produced at trial fit the crimes charged against the defendant, and whether they believe beyond a reasonable doubt that the defendant committed the crimes charged. If the jury believes that the state has proved its case, then it will find the defendant guilty. In most states, the verdict must be unanimous, and this applies to both guilty and not guilty verdicts. Once the jury has reached a verdict, the judge will enter the judgment of conviction. Contrary to popular belief, most jury trials result in the conviction of the defendant on at least one charge.

HUNG JURY

When a jury is unable to agree on a verdict, it is called a *hung jury* and the judge will declare a *mistrial*. The state will have another opportunity (if it chooses) to try the defendant again. If the jury agrees that the evidence presented did not prove beyond a reasonable doubt that the defendant is guilty, the jury can render a verdict of not guilty. In this case, the state cannot retry the defendant again because to do so would violate the Constitutional protection against *double jeopardy* (i.e., being tried twice for the same crime).

THE BENCH TRIAL

If it has been a bench trial, (i.e., tried without a jury), then the judge *takes the case under advisement* and *deliberates* on the facts presented by the state and the defendant. After some consideration of the facts and the law, the judge renders a verdict in the case.

VERDICT ON LESS THAN ALL CHARGES

The prosecutor may have charged several offenses for the acts committed by the defendant. The proof at trial may have convinced a jury that the defendant was guilty of only one or some of the charges, and a finding of guilt would be made on only those charges.

Sometimes, the defendant is found guilty of a *lesser included offense*, which means that the defendant committed a crime, but not the highest offense charged. For example, the defendant is charged with murder which requires proving that the defendant: (1) killed the victim, and (2) did so with the intent to cause death. The jury believes that the defendant did kill the victim, but that the defendant only intended to frighten the victim, not to kill him.

Because the law requires both elements for a finding of guilt on the murder charge, but only one is present, the jury may find the defendant guilty of a lesser included offense such as *manslaughter* (defined as the unintentional killing of a person).

THE SENTENCE 13

Sentencing generally serves three purposes: punishment, deterrence, and rehabilitation. Federal sentencing guidelines apply to federal cases, and each state has the right to design its sentencing scheme. States may follow an *indeterminate* sentencing scheme in which the judge sentences the defendant to a range of years, but the parole board may release the defendant after a certain period of time.

Example: If the judge sentences a defendant to three years to life, the parole board can release the defendant upon a showing of rehabilitation even if the offender has not yet served the minimum length of time.

In a *determinate* scheme, the range of sentence is established by state law and the judge may sentence the defendant within that range. Parole is not available for defendants in a determinate sentencing scheme, so that a defendant would be sentenced for a set period, for example, ten years, and would be required by law to serve a minimum set portion of that sentence.

SENTENCING DISPOSITIONS

Every state has a specific sentencing code that sets forth the range of sentence dispositions for each crime. Some states permit the death penalty for certain types of murder; other states permit up to life in prison. Many states are adopting *truth in sentencing* laws that increase the time served by repeat offenders, and "three strikes and you're out" laws, which require life imprisonment for a "career" criminal upon the third conviction.

Most states permit a range of penalties for the same class of crime. For example, a home invasion and a criminal sexual assault may fall within the same offense classification, with the same potential sentencing range. Generally, the following dispositions exist (these are explained in more detail below):

- execution (in some states);

- imprisonment (including periodic, "boot camp," etc.);

- probation (possibly with home confinement, electronic monitoring, etc.);

- supervision;

- restitution; and

- fine.

EXECUTION   The most serious penalty available is the death penalty (capital punishment). A number of states permit this punishment after a conviction of its highest class of murder, or murder with special circumstances.

As of the year 2000, 38 states permit capital punishment.

Alabama	Nebraska
Arizona	Nevada
Arkansas	New Hampshire
California	New Jersey
Colorado	New Mexico
Connecticut	New York
Delaware	North Carolina
Florida	Ohio
Georgia	Oklahoma
Idaho	Oregon
Illinois	Pennsylvania
Indiana	South Carolina
Kansas	South Dakota

Kentucky	Tennessee
Louisiana	Texas
Maryland	Utah
Mississippi	Virginia
Missouri	Washington
Montana	Wyoming

Every person currently on death row was convicted of murder. In 1999, 98 men in 20 States were executed. Ninety-four of these executions were carried out by lethal injection, 3 by electrocution, and 1 by lethal gas.

IMPRISONMENT

A jail or prison sentence may be mandatory for certain crimes. The maximum length of term is for the defendant's natural life, but some states provide for an indefinite term (1 to 100 years), while others require a definite term (299 years) to be imposed. Some states permit an extended term for exceptionally brutal or heinous behavior, or for repeat offenders.

States may also permit or require sentences to be imposed *concurrently* (at the same time) or *consecutively* (one after the other) if necessary to protect the public. Offenders sentenced to prison will be in the custody of the state's department of corrections, which determines what prison the offender is sent to and whether the offender is transferred.

Boot Camp. In recent years, *boot camps* have become popular for certain types of offenders. Boot camps are also called *impact incarceration*. They have eligibility requirements and many states exclude the most serious crimes or repeat offenders from the program. Boot camps usually last four to six months and require physical training and labor.

Periodic imprisonment. Periodic imprisonment means that the offender will be released during some portion of the sentence and will be confined during the remainder. For example, an offender might spend weekends in jail, but continue to work and support his or her family during the week. Alternatively, a court may sentence the offender to spend one weekend per month in jail for the duration of the sentence imposed.

PROBATION

Crimes that include *probation* as an option tend to be less serious offenses. The possible length of probation varies with the crime charged. A sentence of probation means that the offender is convicted of the crime, but is permitted to remain in the community subject to certain conditions.

Probation may also include some term of periodic imprisonment or community service as part of the sentence. Even if the crime permits probation, a judge can refuse to grant it if the judge believes that the crime charged requires some length of incarceration.

Conditions of probation usually include that the offender:

- not commit any crime;

- report to a probation officer;

- not possess a dangerous weapon;

- not leave the state without the court's permission; and

- not associate with other convicted people.

In addition, the court can impose other conditions on the offender, and some states require a court to impose certain conditions based on the offense.

Example: In a child sexual abuse case where the offender is the father of the victim, a judge who awards probation to the offender may also order the offender to pay for the counseling or other expenses of the victim, or to pay for support of the victim during the length of probation.

Courts often require the defendant to obtain some kind of counseling in domestic violence cases. Many courts order the defendant to have no contact with the victim during the period of probation. Some may require the defendant to obtain drug or alcohol treatment, and to refrain from taking alcohol or illegal drugs.

Intensive probation supervision. California and several other states have experimented with a program of probation commonly called *intensive probation supervision*. This type of program is usually designed for offenders who need closer monitoring than the average probationer. It usually involves electronic home confinement that permits an offender to leave home only for specified reasons such as to attend school or counseling.

SUPERVISION	For minor offenses, where the defendant pleads guilty or stipulates to the facts, the court may order supervision for a period of time, usually a few months, and defer further proceedings in the case. If the defendant serves the period of supervision without committing another offense, the proceedings will be dismissed and no conviction will be entered. You may also hear this referred to as *withheld adjudication*.
RESTITUTION	*Restitution* is ordering the defendant to pay the victim for his or her economic losses. The consideration of ordering restitution is a requirement in some states, and is available whether the defendant is incarcerated or on probation. Even where restitution is not mandatory, the judge can consider restitution for the victim's losses. The victim's request for restitution should be made in the victim impact statement. In a few states, restitution is enforceable as a civil lien or judgment. Although restitution typically does not cover the complete range of claims a crime victim may have as a result of the victimization, by enforcing a civil lien or judgment the victim can proceed with collection immediately after the criminal case, rather than having to begin the process again through the civil courts. Thus, this might be pursued to avoid having to file a civil suit.
FINES	All courts can order the defendant to pay a fine as a condition of probation, and many fines are mandatorily imposed. Court costs are also chargeable to the offender.

THE SENTENCING HEARING

Unless it is a minor case, or the sentence has been the subject of a plea bargain, the sentencing decision will be made after a sentencing hearing at which witnesses can present evidence.

PRESENTENCE INVESTIGATION	After the verdict has been entered, the judge will usually continue the case for a few weeks for a *presentence investigation* to be completed, and for the state and defendant to prepare evidence as to what they believe the appropriate sentence should be. To determine what sentence to impose, the judge weighs several factors, including the severity of the crime and the defendant's criminal history. The court also weighs the harm suffered by the victim.

Special rules for sentencing hearings allow the judge to consider more information as *evidence* than would have been permitted in the trial, such as testimony or letters from any person who has information about the defendant's character, previous history or record of crimes, or any other information that is relevant to the issue of sentencing.

Example: Past victims of a serial rapist can testify at the sentencing hearing to show the defendant's dangerous nature and past criminal history, where they would not be allowed to testify at the trial.

THE PRESENTENCE REPORT

A *presentence report*, usually prepared by a probation or parole agency, helps the court to consider several factors prior to imposing its sentence. For example, if the crime permits a sentence of probation, the presentence investigation would identify whether the defendant is an appropriate candidate, or whether special conditions should be imposed. Among other information, a presentence report can include victim impact information.

THE VICTIM IMPACT STATEMENT

Victims in all states have the right to provide information to the court, for consideration in sentencing, on how the crime has affected them. A formal *victim impact statement* may be the only time that the victim is able to speak to the judge about what has happened to him or her as a result of the crime. Where the victim has died as a result of the crime, or is a minor or incapacitated, it may be the only time that the court hears what impact the crime has had upon the victim's survivors.

In some states this information can be provided to the judge directly; in others, it must be written in a victim impact statement and made part of the presentence investigation provided to the court prior to sentencing. The victim may also be able to present the information orally at the sentencing hearing.

PREPARING THE VICTIM IMPACT STATEMENT

Some states require the victim to prepare the victim impact statement in conjunction with the prosecutor. If the victim is unable to present it in person, it may be able to be presented in writing by the prosecutor at the hearing. If the victim is a young child, the parents of the child may be able to prepare the statement.

In a victim impact statement, you should make sure to explain to the court how the crime has impacted you as well as the other members of your family or household. The statement should cover your emotions as well as any physical suffering as a result of the crime. The statement should also include an explanation of the financial losses you have incurred as a result of the crime. In some states, your opinion as to the defendant's sentence is permitted; in others it is not.

If no form is available, ask your victim assistance advocate or prosecutor for a sample to guide you. Keep your statement to a reasonable length, so that you can present the most important points to the judge. (For a sample victim impact statement form, see form D in Appendix D.)

PRESENTING A
VICTIM IMPACT
STATEMENT IN
COURT

In addition to preparing a victim impact statement, many states allow the victim or victim's representative to present the statement in court at the sentencing hearing. In such cases, the statement is treated like other evidence, and the defendant is entitled to cross-examine the victim at the hearing.

WHAT TO
EXPECT

The sentencing hearing will be like a mini-trial, except that it should be concluded in a much shorter time period. In most cases, a single appearance in court will be sufficient to complete the process, but sometimes the hearing will have to be continued if all of the information that the judge must consider prior to making the decision has not been gathered.

WHAT THE SENTENCE REALLY MEANS

Be aware that despite the truth in sentencing reforms sweeping through the country, often the prison sentence handed out by the judge is not exactly what the offender will actually serve. Over the years, time off for good behavior has become a standard, and an offender will usually serve only part of the actual sentence imposed if he or she behaves while in prison.

Another problem occurs when the offender is sent back to the community to a *half-way house* or with electronic home confinement. This prisoner may still be considered to be in *custody* even though he or she is back in the community and you may be shocked because you were never notified.

Make sure that you have contact with the prosecutor after the sentence is imposed, to get an explanation in clear terms as to what the sentence really means. Find out what office or department will monitor the defendant during the sentence. Get the name, telephone number, and address of the supervising official from the prosecutor.

VIOLATIONS OF SENTENCING ORDERS

An offender who violates his or her sentence of probation, conditional discharge, or parole can be subject to a possible loss of freedom. For example, if the offender was ordered to stay away from the victim as a condition of probation, but follows the victim, the offender is in violation of his or her release conditions. Notify the police immediately, and request the prosecutor to charge the offender with the violation.

Once the violation is reported, the prosecutor can schedule a *revocation* hearing. If he or she has not been arrested for the violation, the offender is served with a summons or subpoena to appear in court. At the hearing, the state must show that the defendant violated a condition of his or her probation in order for the judge to revoke or modify the probation. Failure to pay a restitution order or fine is not usually grounds for revocation of probation, unless the offender willfully refuses to pay.

APPEAL 14

WHO APPEALS

In most criminal cases, the defendant appeals. If the defendant is found guilty, the defendant will often appeal. The prosecution has a limited right to appeal. For example, if the jury acquits the defendant, the defendant's right to avoid *double jeopardy*—being tried twice for the same crime—means the state cannot appeal.

THE OFFENDER DURING AN APPEAL

Although the defendant may have a right to appeal, he or she does not have the same right to be free as prior to trial. The defendant may petition the court for release pending appeal. However, the state will fight this request. In rare cases, a trial judge (or appeals court) may permit the defendant to be free pending the appeals court decision. If so, the same bail conditions may be required, or additional ones can be added pending the outcome of the decision. Once again, if the defendant violates the conditions of his or her release, loss of freedom may be the result.

Make sure you contact the police and your prosecutor to get a copy of the release bond that lists the conditions of bail, and contact the police if you believe the defendant has violated those conditions.

WHAT AN APPEALS COURT CAN DO

Every state has a system of courts designed to hear appeals. No testimony is taken in the appellate process, instead the appeals court simply reviews what happened in the trial to determine if a serious legal error was made. If a serious legal error was made, the conviction can be overturned and the case sent back for a retrial. If a constitutional error was made or if the error cannot be remedied, the conviction may be overturned and the case dismissed. An appeals court can also uphold a conviction, but change the sentence. Appeals are very common in criminal trials, but reversals are rare.

THE VICTIM'S RIGHTS

Victims in many states can request to be informed that an appeal has been filed, and of the status of the appeal. The attorney general's office or a state or local appeals prosecutor will defend the appeal, and the victim can request information from that office. If an appeal includes oral argument, it is a public hearing at which the victim has a right to attend. If you do not know who to contact regarding the appeal, start with the prosecutor or victim-witness assistant who will have (or can find) information for you. Make sure you get a name and contact information to follow-up on the appeals process, which can take several months to a year, or even more.

AFTER THE CRIMINAL TRIAL 15

WHEN IT IS OVER

As you have likely discovered through your journey in the criminal justice system, you are not alone in experiencing the many intense emotions of a victim. Once your case is over, though, you have become a survivor and you can become a resource to others who are just beginning to face this bewildering process.

Contact your local, state, or federal politicians to register your opinion on current legislation or proposals. Contact the media to keep them informed on issues that continue beyond your case.

Example: If you were not afforded your rights under the crime victims rights laws, contact a local newspaper about improving the process for others. If your offender is about to be released back into the community, you can write a letter to your local newspaper or state representative.

Investigate your community and join an organization to speak out for other victims. Become a support person for another victim. Volunteer court-appointed special advocates may be needed by your juvenile or criminal court system to speak for child victims. Some victims have even become activists and have founded organizations dedicated to improving victims rights. Much remains to be done before victims can truly feel that the system was more just than criminal. Find your strength, and your voice, and use them.

RELEASE OR ESCAPE OF THE OFFENDER

The release or escape of a prisoner is of special concern to the victim. Although escape creates an emergency situation that cannot be predicted, the majority of release situations are determined by early release policies of parole boards and corrections officials. The Governor of each state also has the power to commute a prisoner's sentence or pardon a prisoner.

In some states, the offender is eligible for parole, but the trend is to require more offenders to serve a pre-determined length of sentence prior to release. Even if the sentence is preset, *day-for-day good time* permits most prisoners to serve only part of the sentence imposed.

Recently, states have begun enacting registration and notification laws, primarily for sex offenders. By 1998 all states have centralized sex offender registries in operation. Under these schemes, offenders are required to register with authorities upon release, and the public, including victims, can be notified. Some states are enacting *predator laws* for repeat offenders who have not been rehabilitated. These laws permit incarceration for an additional period after the sentence is completed to protect the public.

FINDING OUT ABOUT THE RELEASE

Many states permit the victim some information on the prisoner's status. In most cases, the victim must specifically request this information and provide the appropriate corrections officials with a current address and phone number to receive this information. Write a letter to the department of corrections or parole board requesting to be kept informed of any procedures that may affect the prisoner's status, including release or transfer for work or furlough. See form C in Appendix D for a sample letter.

PRESENTING A VICTIM IMPACT STATEMENT

Some states permit the victim to provide a victim impact statement or appear at the parole hearing to object to the release. This right is especially important, because the parole board does not hear the same evidence and testimony as the trial judge in making its decision. Be sure to update your victim impact statement prepared at the sentencing hearing with how the crime has continued to affect your life and the lives of your family and loved ones. The victim's impact statement and testimony may be very compelling, and public opinion has shaped the willingness of parole officials to grant early release of prisoners.

EMERGING TECHNOLOGY AND CRIME VICTIMS 16

As technology improves, so does the government's efforts to deal with crime and criminals. This technology can be used to help prevent crime; it can also make it easier to learn about crime and criminals. For example, federal, state and local governments have begun to use the World Wide Web to provide an enormous amount of crime information to anyone with access to the Internet. Technology can also assist victims to participate in their cases: a telephone may enable you to register for automatic notice of your pending court case or to be notified automatically of an offender's escape or release from prison. Also, agencies that provide services to crime victims can now be found in great numbers on the Web. (See Appendix A for a list of websites).

With access to the Internet, crime mapping can tell you the crime story of a neighborhood at a glance. You may also be able to find out where the registered sex offenders live or the status of an incarcerated convict. But not all is positive about new technology. Cybercrimes and sexual exploitation of children are two of the negative sides of increased access to the Internet.

VICTIM PARTICIPATION

Technology can help victims participate in their cases.

Example: In the Oklahoma bombing of April, 1995, in which 168 victims died and over 500 more were injured, new technology allowed victims in Oklahoma to watch the defendants' trials in Colorado on closed-circuit television.

Closed-circuit television has also been used to assist child victims in testifying to their abuse. Technology is also helping domestic violence victims. Cellular phones, house perimeter alarms, and electronic bracelets (which limit or track offender's movements) can help protect victims of domestic violence or stalking.

AUTOMATED VICTIM INFORMATION AND NOTIFICATION

The victim's rights laws in every state provide that victims have a right to *notice* and *information* of criminal justice proceedings in their case. (See Appendix C for a summary of state victim's rights laws.) Notice has, in the past, been by telephone call or letter mailed to the victim's last known address. Sometimes, victims had to specifically request information.

Today, new technology has improved the victim's right to know.

Example: When a victim in Kentucky was shot to death in 1994 by her offender who had been released from jail without notice to her, Kentucky responded by automating victim information and making it available to victims through a telephone call.

The federal government is in the process of adopting an automated victim notification system for federal cases, and by the end of 2000, nearly 40 states provided automated victim notification for state cases.

Most automated victim notification programs are similar. The technology works by accessing information from prosecutors, court clerks, and jails or prisons, and then downloading the information into databases. The program only requires that the victim have access to a telephone to use it. After some general information, the caller is asked for the offender's name or state criminal identification number. The program can provide the offender's custody status, including whether he or she has escaped, and provide court dates, times, locations, and continuances. In addition, victims can usually call the system on a toll-free number. Information is normally provided in a number of languages.

After obtaining the offender's court and custody status, the caller can register a telephone number that will be automatically called to provide notice of changes in status, such as when the offender is released or transferred back into the community. Some programs can also provide information through an automatic notification letter to a registered victim.

More information on automated victim notification can be found by calling VINE, the company that provides notification systems in 35 states (and other countries) at 800-865-4314 and asking for the phone number for a participating VINE program in your area. Your jurisdiction may not use VINE as its vendor, so you may also do a search for "automated victim notification" in your jurisdiction on the Internet or contact your local police, prosecutor, or state's attorney general's office for more information.

CRIME MAPPING

Victimization by crime may lead victims to increased sensitivity and awareness of crime rates. Some victims, attacked in their home or whose home was broken into, may choose to move away from the area or scene of the crime. *Crime mapping* can provide a snapshot of crime in a community and assist in evaluating the general safety record of a neighborhood.

Police departments have been using crime maps to analyze crime since the early 1900s, but most recently technology has improved to permit police and other law enforcement agencies to put crime reports online through crime mapping.

Today, larger police departments make available to the public online localized crime information from their crime maps. An Internet user can find out, for example, how many arrests were made for drunk driving in the last month in a particular location (e.g., street, city, or county). On the Chicago Police Department's crime map website, there are maps, graphs, and tables of reported crime for the previous 90 days. It can be searched by street address as well as police districts and schools. Various types of crime reports can be found and mapped out for the user.

Putting crime information online can provide crime victims with valuable information, however, victims also need to be aware that law enforcement records may also contain private information about them. Some states do provide that certain private victim information is not to be included in a public record, other states allow the court to order that certain information be kept private. Check with your police department or prosecutor for more information, or check the law in your own state (See Appendix C).

For more information about police departments with crime maps on the Web, you can visit the crime mapping research center website at the National Institute of Justice at:

http://www.ojp.usdoj.gov/cmrc.

SEX OFFENDERS AND SEXUAL PREDATORS

SEX OFFENDERS

Many sex offenders repeat their crimes. To address the threat of repeat offenders, in the 1990s, states began to track the whereabouts of sex offenders through sex offender registration laws. These laws required certain sex offenders to register with their local police departments when they were released from prison. But, there was no mechanism for letting the community know, which, in part, led to a case that changed the way we deal with these offenders.

On July 29, 1994, Jesse Temmendeqous, just released from a six year sentence for child molestation, lured seven-year-old Megan into his home in New Jersey, promising to show her his puppy. Instead, he sexually assaulted and murdered her. Unbeknownst to the neighborhood, Temmendeqous had moved in with two other convicted child molesters right across the street from Megan.

The outrage over Megan's case was the catalyst for "Megan's Law," passed in New Jersey, which requires paroled sex offenders to give notice to a community prior to their arrival. The requirements of community notification differ from state to state. In over half the states, community notification is permitted for specific types of offenders, such as serial rapists and child sexual offenders, and sexual predators. Notification methods include: sending or posting fliers in the offender's residential area, neighborhood notification by police, community meetings and through the news.

In 1998, the federal government began assisting states in making sure that their sex offender registries are compatible with the FBI's National

Sex Offender Registry file so that state registry information on sex offenders can be obtained and tracked from one jurisdiction to another.

As of 1999, over half of all states have or are developing an Internet site with sex offender registration information on it. Some states have searchable databases with individual sex offender information. A few states also have a sex offender information hot line. (For a state by state summary of notification procedures, see Devon B. Adams, Summary of State Sex Offender Registry Dissemination Procedures, Update 1999 Individual State Summaries, U.S. Department of Justice, Office of Justice Programs, Bureau of Justice Statistics (August 1999) available online at **http://www.ncjrs.org/**).

Because of the threat that sex offenders present, states have also begun using developments in scientific technology to try to solve sexual crimes cases. DNA databases of sex offenders exist, which can match DNA of certain convicted offenders with that collected in unsolved cases.

PREDATORS
Sexual predators have become the newest focus of legal attention in the trend to address the problem of repeat sex offenders. By the late 1990s states had begun to revise their sexual predator laws to address the most dangerous sex offenders. By 1999, at least 17 states permitted continued incarceration of a sex offender at the end of his or her original sentence and until the offender no longer presents a danger to the community. For additional information on this alternative to release, check with your local prosecutor or state Attorney General's office.

CYBERCRIME

New technology is not always positive, and new methods of committing crime are making their way onto the Internet. One type of crime that is becoming the subject of national attention is the exploitation of children online. Another involves what has been called "identity theft" in which the criminal steals the identity of the victim and begins using the victim's name, address, or credit information.

CHILD
EXPLOITATION
ONLINE
Exploiting children through the Internet has become a past-time of online sexual predators who use their computers and the Internet to obtain photographs of child pornography. These offenders also exchange names and addresses of other predators and of potential child-victims.

The Internet also allows these online predators to enter the home of a child who is using a computer. Children may believe they are "chatting" with someone their own age and may share private information about themselves and their families. The predators attempt to develop an online relationship with the child, then attempt to meet the child somewhere in person. Children may not wish to report the contacts to parents because they do not wish to lose their online privileges.

In 1998, the National Center for Missing and Exploited Children began a national clearinghouse for tips and leads regarding the sexual exploitation of children. More information on this issue can be obtained from the National Center at **http://www.missingkids.com**. Reports can be made on-line at: **http://www.missingkids.com/cybertip**, or on the 24-Hour Child Pornography Tipline at 800-843-5678.

IDENTITY THEFT

Although fraudulent use of another's identity occurred before the Internet became popular, technology has made it much easier for this type of thief to steal. The most common types of identity theft are:

- stealing credit information to open or use a credit card in the victim's name;

- fraudulently obtaining a cellular phone account or other utility account; or

- opening a bank account, with the victim's information.

On average, the victim only learns of the theft about 14 months after their identity was stolen.

In 1998, the federal government made identity theft a federal crime, and the majority of states have also passed laws criminalizing identify theft. The Federal Trade Commission (FTC), which began the Identity Theft Hotline and Clearinghouse of information in November of 1999, estimates that in the year 2000 alone, there were over 45,000 calls from victims of identity theft. The FTC has published a booklet on identity theft that explains the steps that a victim should take upon learning of the theft. (See FTC, "ID Theft, When Bad Things Happen To Your Good Name," available by calling 877-IDTHEFT or you may go to the Identity Theft Clearinghouse website at:

http://www.consumer.gov/idtheft/

RECOVERING DAMAGES 17

While the focus of the criminal case is concerned with punishing the offender and deterring the offender from committing further crimes, it is not concerned with the victim's individual welfare. The victim may have lost time off of work, have pain and suffering, and may even have lost a house or job while trying to seek justice in the criminal case. The focus of the civil case is to compensate the victim/plaintiff. The plaintiff in a civil suit can find out about the assets of the defendant and literally take away the defendant's profits that he may have made on the crime. The losses suffered by the plaintiff are the "damages" in a civil suit.

CRIMINAL VERSUS CIVIL COURT

The world of civil suits is completely different from the criminal justice system. The rules and procedures may sound similar, but they operate very differently in civil court. For example, the parties in the criminal case are the State, represented by the prosecutor, on behalf of the victim and all of the people in that state; and the defendant represented by his attorney or appointed counsel if he cannot afford his own attorney. The victim is merely a witness in criminal court, but in filing a civil suit, the victim is in control.

The parties in a civil suit are the *plaintiff* (victim), who may be represented by an attorney, and the *defendant* (the offender or a third party), who may also be represented by counsel. As a party, the victim can make all the decisions that the prosecutor could make in the criminal case. Because a civil suit is a private action, no attorneys will be appointed. If either party wants an attorney, they must hire their own counsel.

STANDARD OF PROOF

One difference between criminal and civil cases is the standard of proof required for the judge or jury to find against the defendant. In the civil case, the plaintiff must prove, usually by a *preponderance of the evidence* that the defendant caused the injuries for which the plaintiff is entitled to damages. In the criminal case, the prosecutor must prove *beyond a reasonable doubt* that the offender committed the crime for which he is charged. These standards are general concepts, not precise definitions, but the criminal standard is much higher and harder to meet than the civil standard. The civil standard of a preponderance of the evidence has been described as requiring the jury to find that the plaintiff's version of the facts is slightly more likely than the defendant's version. It has also been described as requiring the plaintiff to prove his case by slightly more than a 50% certainty.

Although it is difficult to compare the two standards in terms of a percentage, it has been said that *beyond a reasonable doubt* requires at least a 75% certainty, because some states allow convictions based upon the agreement of nine out of twelve jurors. Jurors are often instructed by the judge that if they are to find the defendant not guilty, they should have a doubt that is based upon logic and reason. A juror can have some doubt, and still convict. The standard is not beyond *all* doubt, or beyond *a shadow* of a doubt.

COMPELLING THE DEFENDANT'S TESTIMONY

Further, there is no right of the defendant to avoid the witness stand in civil court as he could do in criminal court. So the plaintiff can require the defendant to testify, and may be able to ask those questions that could not be asked of the defendant in criminal court.

NOTE: *The chart on the following page shows some of the differences between the criminal and civil systems.*

Comparison of Criminal and Civil Court Systems

	CIVIL	CRIMINAL
Parties	Victim=Plaintiff v. Defendant=Criminal or Third Party	State v. Defendant
Goal of the Case	Compensate Plaintiff; punish Defendant monetarily	Rehabilitate, punish & deter Defendant
Who Benefits	Plaintiff	People or society at large
Standard of Proof	Preponderance of the evidence (more likely than not)	Beyond a reasonable doubt (highest standard required)
Evidence	Inquiry very broad; Defendant generally must answer Plaintiff's questions	Defendant has Constitutional right not to testify or answer questions
Verdicts	In favor of Plaintiff, or in favor of Defendant	Guilty; Not guilty; Guilty but insane; Mistrial
Judgment	Compensate Plaintiff for losses, and punish Defendant monetarily	Defendant is punished through a sentence
Outcomes	Judgment for Plaintiff and punish Defendant monetarily; no damages awarded	Defendant sentenced to prison, jail, probation; pays restitution to victim, or fine to State
Settlement	Plaintiff chooses when and for how much	Prosecutor chooses to negotiate; Victim cannot prevent settlement

OTHER OPTIONS FOR RECOVERY OF DAMAGES

CRIME VICTIM
COMPENSATION

All states have set up a fund to compensate victims of crime. Each state sets out eligibility requirements and generally requires that victims report promptly, cooperate with the police and file a claim within a certain period of time. In addition to a civil suit, a victim should seek an award of compensation from the state crime victim's compensation fund. In most states, eligible victims can be compensated for out-of-pocket losses resulting from the crime. Where a victim later recovers damages in the civil suit, state law may require that the victim's compensation program be reimbursed from the civil damage award.

RESTITUTION AND
REPARATION

As part of the criminal sentence, the offender may be ordered to pay *restitution*, sometimes called *reparation*. Although these terms do differ slightly, they generally reach the same result. Usually, restitution is ordered for those offenders who receive probation, but some states mandate restitution be ordered regardless of the type of sentence imposed. This remedy is limited to those offenders who have the ability to pay and usually to actual out-of-pocket losses suffered by the victim. An order of restitution does not affect the victim's right to file a civil suit, but may be deducted from the recovery awarded.

INSURANCE

Insurance may cover some of the losses. For example, auto insurance will cover theft or criminal damage to a vehicle and its contents, while homeowner's insurance provides similar coverage for loss to contents in the home. Medical insurance may reimburse the victim for medical and hospital expenses for injuries resulting from the crime.

The What and Who of a Civil Lawsuit

18

The Civil Suit

A *civil suit* is a lawsuit brought by one party against another. When a person is victimized by a crime, that person has the right to file a civil suit to seek damages for the crime. In a civil action, the goal is to compensate the victim; in some cases, the suit may also result in punishing the wrongdoer.

NOTE: *An indepth discussion of civil suits is beyond the scope of this book. Either obtain a book on the topic or contact an attorney if you decide to file a civil suit.*

ADVANTAGES AND
DISADVANTAGES

In the civil case, the plaintiff chooses who to sue and for what reason. The plaintiff can decide to settle the case, and the amount that he or she is willing to accept for a settlement. But a civil suit is not quick. Even simple civil suits may take upwards of a year to complete; some can take as long as four years.

Nor is a civil suit judgment an automatic award of money. The judgment is written on a piece of paper, but if the defendant is *judgment proof*, (i.e., he is indigent, has no assets, or has hidden his assets well), then collecting the judgment may be impossible. In some cases, the defendant may be in jail for a long time, so the judgment may have to be held and renewed in the event the defendant inherits, wins, or earns sufficient assets to pay the damages.

THE PARTIES TO THE SUIT

THE PLAINTIFF
The *plaintiff* is the person who files the suit. Generally, the plaintiff, as the directly injured party, will be the crime victim. Other plaintiffs can include the victim's spouse, parents, or other family members who have suffered certain losses as a result of the crime. If the victim dies during the commission of the crime or as a result of the crime, then the plaintiffs might be his or her estate and surviving family members, who will usually be able to seek recovery for the *wrongful death* of the victim.

THE DEFENDANT
The plaintiff may have several choices of *defendant* in a civil suit. Choosing the defendant (or defendants) requires consideration of the goals of the lawsuit. Of course, the obvious defendant is the criminal offender. However, if the criminal is never caught or has no assets with which to pay damages, then filing a suit against the offender will not result in funds to compensate the victim's losses. If a third party is a possible defendant, he or she may have sufficient assets or insurance coverage to adequately compensate the plaintiff's losses.

The Offender. The plaintiff may seek damages from the offender. The civil suit may be filed regardless of whether the offender has been charged in criminal court.

Multiple Offenders. If the conduct of two or more persons caused the injury, the victim can sue any one, or all of them.

Example: Joint liability may exist where only one of the assailants slashes the tires on the victim's car, while the others helped to drive or acted as lookouts. Each wrongdoer may be held liable for the entire damage award.

Juvenile Offenders. Generally, children under seven years of age can be held liable for intentional acts that form the basis of the criminal charge (but not for negligent acts). Even if the minor is not charged, a civil case may still be filed on the intentional act, but it may be limited depending upon the age of the child, and whether the conduct was reckless or negligent instead of intentional. Between the ages of seven and fourteen, a child can be found liable for negligence, but the jury will measure his conduct be special standards (i.e., his experience, age, and mental capacity). Mentally incompetent persons are viewed similarly to children over age seven.

FAMILY
MEMBERS
If the criminal act was an intentional act committed by a spouse or other family member, a lawsuit against the family member is generally allowed. This is not true for reckless or negligent acts, as some states will not permit such suits, based on the doctrine of "intra-familial" or "intra-spousal" immunity (the purpose of this doctrine is to maintain good relations in families, and to prevent family members from getting together on a scheme to obtain money from their insurance carrier).

THIRD PARTIES
In addition to criminal charges, a lawsuit may also be filed against any person, agency, organization, corporation, or other entity that allowed the injury to occur through negligence or willful and wanton misconduct. Today, it is common in crime victim litigation to see a third party as a defendant.

Example: An employer who fails to use reasonable care in screening, supervising, or retaining a school bus driver who molests a child on the bus, may be held liable for creating the condition which led to the child's injuries. Or an apartment complex owner may be held liable to a rape victim for failing to provide adequate parking lot lighting or security.

DEFENDANT'S SUIT AGAINST THE VICTIM

While the criminal case is pending, the criminal may file suit against the victim in an effort to intimidate the victim into dropping criminal charges. Although the defendant may have the right to file a case, all states have laws that protect victims from intimidation by the defendant. Make sure that you notify the prosecutor immediately of any attempt to intimidate you. The criminal can face new charges based on intimidation of a witness. If the case has been completed, the offender may still harass the victim by filing suit after he is convicted and sent to prison. Courts understand the attempts to intimidate and harass victims and while some cases are successful, nearly all reported cases have been dismissed upon request of the victim.

THE BURDEN OF PROOF

The plaintiff has the burden to prove all the elements of the lawsuit, but because this is a civil case, the burden of proof is not as strict as the *beyond a reasonable doubt* of the criminal case. In a civil case, the burden is said to be a *preponderance of the evidence*, which means there is enough evidence to make it more likely than not that the defendant did the things he or she is said to have done. If so, the plaintiff has sufficiently met the burden of proof.

THEORIES—TORTS

When a crime victim files a civil suit seeking damages for personal injury or damage to property, the basis for the lawsuit is found in tort law. A *tort* is committed when one, through his wrongful conduct, injures another. In other words, just as a crime is a public wrong, a tort is a private wrong. For every crime there is a tort remedy against the criminal for the injured victim. Most cases allege several theories and seek recovery on as many bases as the facts will support.

Tort law is broader than criminal law. In addition to the intentional criminal conduct of the offender, any person or organization that failed to meet its responsibilities to the victim may also be held liable for the victim's injuries. The duty is usually said to be one of *reasonable care*, or something a reasonable person would or would not do under the circumstances. Duties can be imposed by a state law, municipal ordinance, administrative regulation, industry standard, or even through the common practices and procedures developed throughout the years.

Example: A landlord who is required by local ordinance to keep the property free of dangerous hazards has a duty to meet that standard for the tenants of the building. If the landlord fails to provide adequate lighting on the property, which permits the criminal to hide out, stalk and injure the victim, the landlord may be held liable for contributing to the condition that caused the injury.

THEORIES—CRIMES

Most cases against the offender allege his intentional conduct as the basis for the suit. There are numerous legal theories that are available to crime victims. These include:

- *assault* (threats);

- *battery* (physical injury);

- *false imprisonment* (detention of the victim);,

- *property damage*;

- *trespass*;

- *theft*;

- *intentional infliction of emotional distress*;

- *rape*;

- *sexual assault*; and

- *wrongful death*.

If the offender is a professional or an employer, there are several additional bases to support the suit, such as *malpractice*. Further, if the offender is a parent, *parental negligence* may be added.

Assault, for example, includes apprehension, fear, and intimidation as the basis for the assault case. So, when the defendant raises his hand to strike, but stops short, an assault is committed even where there is no contact. And pointing a gun at the victim (even though the victim did not know it was unloaded) would constitute an assault. However, words alone are not usually sufficient for an assault, unless some other circumstances exists that create a reasonable apprehension of immediate physical contact.

Battery is a very common element of many crime victims' civil suits. This includes a whole range of physical contact, from mere touching to severe violence, and includes both direct and indirect contact. Kicking the victim is a battery, and so is kicking away the victim's cane, because physical contact was indirectly made with the victim.

Interference with the victim's property can also be the subject of a civil suit. This includes vandalism, trespass, or damaging or destroying property.

THEORIES—THIRD PARTIES

If a third party had a special relationship with the victim, there may be additional theories based on negligence, including parental negligence, professional malpractice, failure to maintain the premises, or negligence in hiring or retaining an employee. For example, an employer who fails to complete a legally mandated background criminal history check on a new daycare center worker with a prior criminal conviction for molesting children, may be responsible to the child and the parents of the child who had a right to expect the employer to follow the law.

Each civil lawsuit has a number of required elements that must be proven in order to be successful. The crime victim who files a civil lawsuit is treated no differently than any other plaintiff who comes before a civil court. Knowledge of these basic elements is essential to understanding the documents that must be prepared and filed prior to presenting the case to the court.

PROVING THE ELEMENTS OF AN INTENTIONAL TORT

Generally, for *intentional torts*, the plaintiff must prove: (1) an act; (2) causation; and (3) damages. The term *intent* in an intentional tort does not mean an intent to do harm. It simply requires an intent to commit a certain act for which it is foreseeable that certain consequences are likely to occur.

Because a battery is an intentional tort, the defendant must intend to commit the act which causes harm or offense to the plaintiff. Damages are available for physical injuries as well as emotional injuries. The plaintiff may seek recovery for medical bills, lost income and earning capacity, pain and suffering, and any permanent physical or mental injuries.

CAUSATION

THE OFFENDER

The injury must have been caused by the action or inaction of the defendant. In the case of the criminal as the defendant, there is usually no problem in demonstrating that *but for* the acts of the criminal, the victim would not have suffered injury. A judgment of conviction on the criminal charges proving the defendant guilty of the crime (or crimes) can be sufficient to establish the causation element in the civil case. A plea of guilty may also be admissible as evidence of guilt in the civil case.

THIRD PARTIES

Most third party defendants argue, however, that they did not cause the injury to the victim. Their argument is that the criminal's acts were not under their control. And it is true that there is no duty on the part of a third party to control the criminal acts of another. Courts, however, recognize that there can be more than one cause of injury.

Example: The landlord who fails to change the locks on an apartment and allows an assailant easy access to the victim's apartment through the use of an old key, is responsible because the landlord had a special relationship with the victim tenant and failed to take action (change the locks), which contributed to the ability of the criminal to cause the victim's harm.

Often courts use a *foreseeability* test to determine whether a third party, like the landlord, could have foreseen the likelihood of the crime against the victim.

Example: Courts may consider whether there were other crimes committed in the apartment complex or whether another tenant complained to the management of similar criminal activities, which provided notice to the landlord that these criminal acts were likely to occur.

COMMON DEFENSES

The defense of a civil suit will focus on three areas:

1. jurisdiction;
2. parties; and
3. facts.

JURISDICTION   A *jurisdictional* defense may be made when the case is filed in the wrong court, filed beyond the permitted time period, or where the minimum damage requests have not been made.

Example: If state law permits the victim to file the suit in the county either where the crime occurred or where the defendant lives, but the victim files in another county, the suit may be dismissed for improper jurisdiction. Also, if the suit is filed on the basis of the victim's personal injury, the state law may limit the period within which a suit may be filed to a few years. A suit filed after that time would be subject to the defense that the court does not have jurisdiction over a suit filed after the permitted limitations period.

Finally, some courts have damage request thresholds that must be met by including it in the initial pleading documents filed with the court.

Example: Suppose the state law provided that, to file in the circuit court, the complaint must seek damages of at least $50,000 (otherwise it must be filed in county district court). A complaint that requests $40,000 would be subject to dismissal on the basis that it did not meet the jurisdictional requirements of the court.

PARTIES   A defense based on the parties will usually be made by a third party defendant. In this defense, the defendant will ask the court to dismiss the case because the complaint fails to properly identify or name the defendant. For example, if the victim lists in the complaint the individual property manager, but the landlord is actually a corporation, the defendant will be improperly named. Some defendants are protected from suit by special statutes. For example, if the defendant is a governmental entity, it may argue that it is protected from suit by special laws granting it *immunity*.

The defendant may argue that the victim provoked the defendant or he may argue self defense and try to put the victim on trial.

FACTUAL   Beyond the technical defenses listed above, defendants commonly raise
DEFENSES   factual defenses. The defendant may argue that the victim contributed to his or her own injuries. If the defendant is the offender and the case involves his intentional criminal conduct, then this defense fails. If the facts support it, the negligent defendant may argue that the victim contributed to causing the injuries, in an effort to reduce a damage award on the basis of the victim's fault.

Example: If the victim failed to take proper care to reasonably protect him or herself from harm, that may be considered in the civil suit. In one case, the judgment award for negligence against the owner of the premises was reduced by 97% upon a finding that the plaintiff, a rape victim, was also negligent when she opened her door to strangers without determining who was there.

DAMAGES

The concept of *damages* is very broad in the civil law. In tort law, each individual is presumed to intend all the natural and probable consequences of his or her deliberate acts, but the specific result need not be foreseeable.

Example: If the victim has a heart attack during a robbery, the criminal/defendant could be held liable even though he could not foresee the death or additional injury to the victim.

An award of damages may be compensatory, punitive, or both. The amount of money to award is a question of fact for the jury or judge. The plaintiff can request a certain amount but the jury or judge may award a greater or lesser amount.

COMPENSATORY DAMAGES

Compensatory damages compensate the victim for tangible losses. Compensatory damages provide recovery for physical injury and resulting medical expenses, earning capacity, and pain and suffering. The proof of damages is simple in the case of medical expenses, or bills to repair or replace property, where the victim can show an exact dollar amount of loss. Determining how to put a dollar amount on past and future *pain and suffering* is more challenging. Nonetheless, these *intangibles* can be itemized, and juries and judges make awards everyday that include pain and suffering for victims.

PUNITIVE DAMAGES

Punitive damages may also be awarded to punish the offender or to deter others from engaging in the conduct that led to the offense. Punitive damages are usually awarded only for outrageous or egregious conduct. For intentional conduct, punitive damages may be appropriate. A particular statute may permit punitive damage awards in certain cases. In negligence cases, where the conduct is willful and wanton so as to offend the sensibilities of the public, punitive damages may be awarded. The jury may make a specific award separate from the compensatory damage award.

THE EFFECT OF THE CRIMINAL CASE ON THE CIVIL SUIT

The filing of a civil suit is not dependent on the status of any criminal proceeding. Therefore, the victim can sue at the same time as the criminal case is proceeding; and can also sue if no criminal charges are filed, or if the defendant is not convicted. If the criminal is convicted, evidence of the defendant's guilt can be used in the civil case. Because the burden of proof is higher in a criminal case, more than enough evidence of the criminal's guilt has already been proved in the criminal court. A plea of guilty is admissible in the civil case. In some states, a guilty plea or conviction will establish liability and the only remaining questions will be proof of damages. In others, the defendant will be permitted to explain the reasons for a guilty plea.

Even if the defendant is found not guilty in the criminal case, it will not prevent the victim from filing a civil suit. Because the burden of proof is higher in the criminal case, there may nonetheless be a *preponderance of the evidence*, which would meet the level of proof required for the civil case. In other words, although the evidence was not quite enough for proof beyond a reasonable doubt in the criminal case, it may be enough for the lower standard of proof on a preponderance of the evidence in the civil case. So, an acquittal cannot be used as evidence in the later civil case because it does not prove that the defendant did not commit the crime.

Example: The families of Ron Goldman and Nicole Brown filed civil suits against O.J. Simpson, even though he was found not guilty of their murders in the criminal case. The jury verdict in the criminal case is simply that the prosecutor failed to prove Simpson's guilt beyond a reasonable doubt; not that Simpson proved himself innocent. Therefore, the Goldmans and Browns were still able to prove their civil case on a preponderance of the evidence.

THE EFFECT OF A CIVIL SUIT ON THE VICTIM

Now that you understand the "what" of civil suits, and you are considering your options, be aware of the impact that a civil suit may have on you. Before undertaking what may take years to complete, consider why you want to file and what resolution you would like to see. If you have access to a therapist, discuss your consideration and its potential impact on your health and well-being. Realize that the civil suit will continue the litigation started in the criminal case, and that you may not be able to put the crime behind you for some time to come. Realize, too, that there will be a financial commitment on your part as well as an emotional one.

Consider carefully your willingness to go the distance in seeking justice. Also weigh the possibility that you may not win or collect money damages. If, upon weighing all these factors, you determine to proceed, then commit yourself to the battle and seek the justice you are entitled to in the civil court arena.

During the pendency of the civil suit, be aware of the physical and psychological effect that it has on your well-being. Numerous agencies can offer support and assistance to crime victims. Contact the National Center for Victims of Crime more detailed information on services in you locality (see Appendix A for resource information).

The How and When of a Civil Lawsuit

19

A civil suit filed in any court follows a set of procedural laws and rules that guide the process for the parties to the suit. Federal courts follow the Federal Rules of Civil Procedure. Similarly, each state has its own code of civil procedures and court rules. The parties to a civil suit must follow the procedural rules of the jurisdiction in which the lawsuit is filed in order to proceed with the case. If the lawsuit is a simple one seeking a small amount of damages, all jurisdictions have special *small claims* courts in which plaintiffs may sue, in many cases without a lawyer. If the suit is more complex or seeks a larger damage award, a different set of rules will likely apply. See Appendices B and C for guidance in finding the civil rules of your jurisdiction. For assistance in exploring your rights to file a civil case, you may also choose to contact the National Crime Victim Bar Association at:

703-276-0960 or

http://www.victimbar.org

EVALUATING AND PREPARING THE CASE

Careful preparation is required prior to filing a civil case.

IDENTIFYING AND COLLECTING PROOF

Identification of the proof necessary to successfully prove the claim depends on the facts of the case. What facts does the plaintiff need to prove? What crime was committed against you? Who was at fault for the crime? Who contributed to the circumstances that led up to the crime? What facts exist to prove the crime was committed? What injuries have you suffered as a result of the crime (e.g., financial, emotional, and physical)? How do you find that information? Who can provide information about your case?

Assume your apartment has been burglarized. You call the police and make a report. The burglar is never apprehended, but you learn through the police investigation that several other tenants have made similar break-in reports, and in each instance, the burglar gained access through the broken lock on the back lobby door of the building. Although there have been several similar crimes committed and complaints have been made to the landlord, the landlord has failed to remedy the situation by fixing the door or changing the lock. Through the police investigation on your report, you learn that your burglar also used the broken back lobby door to gain entrance to the building.

In speaking to the police, you may identify several potential witnesses to similar crimes, and you may have learned that the landlord was *on notice* and has failed to take action. Local ordinances or state laws may list certain obligations of the landlord to tenants. For example, perhaps the landlord was required to install deadbolt locks on the outer doors, but has never done so.

Although the property you lost is never recovered, you have a list of the items taken and you have valued those items. You also find that you are unable to sleep at night for fear that the burglar may return again while you are in the apartment. The crime has caused you to experience nightmares and you seek the help of a therapist. Cooperation with the police has caused you to lose days at work and you are forced to use vacation days to cover your losses.

The proof of a civil case will be offered by the plaintiff to support the facts listed in the complaint. Proof may exist in the form of the testimony of a witness or a document that includes information on an element of the civil case.

For example, proof of the commission of the crime may include information gathered by law enforcement personnel. When the police arrived at the scene of the crime, a police report will be completed listing the nature of the call, any witnesses present, any physical evidence of a crime (such as a broken window or pry marks on the door). Often there will also be supplemental reports that investigators or other law enforcement personnel may complete upon speaking to the witnesses or collecting items of proof from the crime scene.

During the prosecution of the criminal case, there will be testimony of witnesses, and the introduction of physical evidence. Most states' victim's rights laws permit the victim to obtain the prompt return of evidence collected from the victim for purposes of criminal prosecution at the end of the case. Usually, however, the victim must make this request. (See Appendix C for your state's laws.)

Proof of the judgment of conviction can be obtained through the clerk of the court in which the criminal conviction was entered. A copy that is certified by the court clerk will usually be required by the civil court.

To prove damages, the plaintiff may use medical or mental health records that document the physical and psychological injuries suffered as a result of the crime. The victim may also use employment records to show lost income, lost benefits, or even loss of a job due to the crime. These records can often be obtained through a written request, or the plaintiff may request a subpoena be issued, ordering the medical doctor, mental health professional, or employer to release information in his or her files.

ORGANIZING THE FACTS | Keeping your facts organized for easy and ready reference is essential in preparing your case. Keep a diary of events from the commission of the crime, listing who you have talked to and what information you have learned, as well as your emotional, physical, and psychological reactions to the crime. If your case is prosecuted, keep a record of the events in the criminal case. Keep all of the bills you incur as a result of the crime.

THE TIME AND PLACE TO FILE

Careful consideration of the proper time to file is also crucial, as all jurisdictions place time limits on access to civil courts. In determining the best time to file suit, the victim should consider that, while the criminal case is pending, the defendant could assert his 5th Amendment privilege not to testify in the civil case. Once the defendant is convicted or acquitted of the crime, he can no longer assert this privilege in the civil case, and therefore can be required to testify and produce evidence.

Because the conviction may be useful to the victim in a civil suit, the victim will likely be questioned during the criminal case about whether a civil suit is pending, to try to show the victim's motive or bias. Also, the criminal investigation may yield important information for the civil case, at no cost to the victim. For these reasons, victims may choose to wait until the completion of the criminal case before filing a civil suit.

STATUTES OF LIMITATION

Although the victim may have some choices to make about when to file the civil suit, all states provide a limitation period within which a personal injury or property loss action must be filed. The laws vary from state to state, but many *statutes of limitation* allow only one or two years within which to file a lawsuit for personal injuries resulting from the crime. California, for example, permits a victim to file a civil suit up to one year after a criminal conviction is entered for a felony crime.

Suits against particular kinds of defendants, like governmental entities, may also have special time limits or notice requirements which are much shorter than the general time limits. Check with the agency directly for any notice or form required to be filed, or check with an attorney familiar with lawsuits against governmental entities. And, although states vary, child victims generally have until they reach the age of majority within which to file a lawsuit. One new trend in child victim cases is that a number of states have recently extended the statute of limitations for adults who were sexually abused as children.

WHERE TO FILE

The choice of where to file the lawsuit will depend on the nature of the case, and the convenience of the plaintiff. The great majority of civil suits are filed in state courts. Often, state rules permit the plaintiff to file for injuries in the court where the crime occurred, or where the plaintiff or defendant reside.

The plaintiff may also be able to file the case in federal court under certain circumstances. The requirements for filing civil cases in federal court can be found in the United States Code Service (U.S.C.S.) reporters. For example, a civil lawsuit may be filed in federal court if the plaintiff can assert claims based on the U.S. Constitution or seeks damages for violation of civil rights (U.S.C.S., Title 22, Sec. 1340). The suit may also be filed in federal court if the plaintiff requests damages in excess of $50,000, and the defendant resides in a different state from the plaintiff (U.S.C.S., Title 28, Sec. 1332). In a few cases, the suit must be filed in federal court, such as where the defendant is an employee of the federal government and the crime occurred while the employee was acting within the scope of his office or employment (U.S.C.S., Title 28, Sec. 1346).

The decision as to proper jurisdiction may be a clear one, but it may also be a very important cross-road in the case. If you are unsure, or your research points to options between state and federal court filings, you would be wise to consult with an attorney who has experience in the type of suit to be filed.

ENFORCING THE JUDGMENT

After you file and go to court, a *judgment* is rendered. If it is in your favor, collection of a judgment amount is the final goal, and may be challenging. Some criminals are *indigent* (i.e., they do not have any real assets from which to draw funds to pay the judgment amount). Other criminals are employed and do have some income. They may own a business or have other property assets which can be used to satisfy a judgment. Also, if the defendant inherits money or wins the lottery, those funds can be used to pay the victim's judgment. Finally, some criminals sue the government or the prison system for *civil rights* violations and recover monies. These can be used to satisfy a judgment in the victim's civil case.

"SON OF SAM" *"Son of Sam"* laws may also provide funds for collection of a victim's judgment. These laws were passed after serial killer David Berkowitz sold the story of his murders for money. Although the laws differ in each state, generally they require the victim to file a claim based on a civil judgment obtained within a certain period of time. When the criminal is convicted and receives profits, that money is then turned over to the state for distribution to the victim. In 1991, however, New York's Son of Sam law was declared unconstitutional because, among other things, it applied too broadly to include persons who had not been accused or convicted of crimes. Check with your State Attorney General's Office to determine the status of the law, and your eligibility to access any such funds in your state.

No Assets
If the defendant does have assets with which to satisfy the judgment but refuses to pay, the plaintiff can return to court to seek enforcement by attaching specific assets. For example, if the defendant is employed, a wage garnishment proceeding can be instituted in which a percentage of the defendant's income is withheld by the defendant's employer and paid directly to the plaintiff. If the defendant has real estate, the court can order confiscation through a *sale and levy* procedure whereby the property is sold at public auction or transferred to the plaintiff to satisfy the judgment.

Bankruptcy
A defendant may seek to avoid collection of a judgment by declaring bankruptcy. Generally, a judgment for intentional conduct is not dischargeable in bankruptcy, but a judgment based on negligence may be discharged. The victim who obtains a judgment will be notified by the Bankruptcy Court if the defendant tries to obtain a discharge. File an *objection* with the Bankruptcy Court to establish that the conduct is not dischargeable.

A defendant may be able to gain some relief from the judgment by filing a type of bankruptcy in which he agrees to pay a percentage of the judgment under a plan approved by a bankruptcy court. In this case, be sure to participate in the creditor's hearing on approval of the defendant's proposed plan of payment to ensure your rights.

THE ROLE OF LAWYERS 20

The role of lawyers in civil suits is completely different than in the criminal justice system. Unlike the criminal case, there is no lawyer involvement in a civil case unless a party hires a lawyer. If you want a lawyer, you will have to hire one or find one who will take the case without charge. Remember that the defendant does not have a right to have a lawyer appointed either.

Recognize that the law is a business as well as a profession. Your decision to hire an attorney may be based on the complexity of your case. Attorneys also make decisions on whether to accept a case based on a number of factors. For example, an attorney is likely to consider the potential for collection from the defendant prior to committing resources towards the case.

In evaluating a case, an attorney will examine:

- cost;

- time and effort; and

- potential for collection.

LAWYERS AND CONFIDENTIALITY

To encourage people to speak freely to their lawyers, the law provides confidentiality protection for clients. This is called the *attorney-client privilege*. The privilege prevents a lawyer from disclosing your information under most circumstances, so be honest in disclosing all the facts, even those facts about the crime or yourself which are embarrassing or humiliating. The lawyer needs this information to properly evaluate the case.

FINDING A LAWYER

The search for a lawyer can take some time and no small amount of perseverance. Just as there are specialities in other professions, it is becoming rarer today to find a lawyer that has a general practice. Many lawyers limit their practice to certain types of cases, such as family law, estate planning, corporate law, etc. The lawyer you choose should have some experience in similar cases, and it would be ideal if he or she had filed a civil suit on behalf of a crime victim prior to your case.

RECOMMENDATIONS FROM FRIENDS

Many times a lawyer is chosen through the help of recommendations by family or friends. These recommendations can be helpful because the good experience of your family member or friend may provide reliable information on the quality of service provided by the lawyer.

REFERRAL SERVICES

If you do not personally know a lawyer and do not have a recommendation from a trusted friend or family member, you can look to other sources. In most cities there is a local *bar association* which is an organization to which many local attorneys will belong. The bar association can help make lawyer referrals, either formally or informally. Sometimes, a recent judgment or settlement of a personal injury lawsuit is publicized and the plaintiff's lawyer's name is listed. Many lawyers now have Web pages on the Internet. Recently, some lawyers have begun to advertise on television or radio. Your victim/witness coordinator or victim advocate from your criminal case may also be able to provide you with resources.

LAW SCHOOL PROGRAMS

One often overlooked resource is a clinic program in a law school. Some law schools maintain programs that take cases of public interest in particular areas. Be sure to check with the law schools in your state to see whether such programs exist and whether your case would qualify. If the clinic accepts your case, you may not be required to pay or your fee will be substantially reduced.

ATTORNEY REGISTRATION

Every state maintains a registration of lawyers who practice law within that state. To find the phone number and address of any lawyer within your state, contact the bar association or other attorney registration office in your state. Look in the phone book, ask your prosecutor (who will also be registered), or contact your state attorney general's office for assistance. To find your local bar association, simply look in the yellow pages for the listing under *"lawyer referrals"*.

INITIAL CONTACT

The selection of a lawyer usually begins with a phone call. In this first contact with the lawyer, be sure to obtain some preliminary information.

- Does this lawyer have experience in your type of case?

- Will you be charged for the first visit?

- How long will you meet for the first visit?

- How much does this lawyer usually charge for services?

Compare the answers given by the lawyers you speak to, then decide which one to meet with for an initial consultation about your case.

FIRST INTERVIEW

The initial interview with a lawyer is very important. Remember that you have not agreed to anything other than the terms of the initial visit. Do not be intimidated by the thought of meeting with the lawyer. You are under no obligation to sign or agree to anything at this time, and you can take any written documents home to think about before you sign. Follow your instincts and trust your evaluation of the person before you. Do you like this lawyer? Do you feel that he or she is listening to you and your story? Are you treated with respect during the visit by the office staff? Your "gut" will tell you much about whether you wish to proceed further with this lawyer.

In telling the lawyer about your case, be as clear and concise as possible. You might write out certain points to be sure you cover the important issues so that the lawyer can properly evaluate your case. Be sure to bring any relevant documents (police reports, court records from the criminal case, etc.) that will help the lawyer to understand your facts.

Discuss what the attorney believes the projected costs to be and how you will be billed for those costs.

Example: If deposition transcripts and expert witnesses are to be retained, are those costs passed on to you or will those persons wait until the end of the case?

FEE AGREEMENTS

It is essential that you understand how the lawyer charges fees and costs. Most attorneys are expensive; charging more than $100 per hour, so sometimes the primary consideration in hiring a lawyer is your ability to pay. In recognition of this limitation, some attorneys who believe the case is meritorious will accept a *contingent fee* arrangement, in which they agree to wait until the end of the case to obtain their fee. The usual agreement states that if there is a judgment, the attorney is entitled to a percentage of the judgment as the fee (usually 1/3 to 40%), but if there is no award of damages, no fee will be due. The plaintiff is still responsible for *costs* (e.g., filing fees, photocopying, telephone charges, postage, transcript, and reporter fees).

Other attorneys charge by the hour up to a certain amount, and require a substantial initial payment from the victim. These attorneys feel that the victim's investment is essential and is a fair balance for the lawyer's consideration, time, and effort. Fees remaining up to a ceiling amount (such as 33% of the recovery) will be due only if there is a judgment or settlement award.

Make sure that you secure your fee agreement in writing so that there will be no confusion as to what is due and when. The agreement should clearly state whether an initial payment is due (sometimes called a *retainer*) and how it should be paid; and whether there is an hourly fee rate charged or a *contingent* fee arrangement. The types of costs and methods by which those costs will be paid should be identified in the agreement.

If a retainer is to be paid, be sure you and your lawyer agree what minimal services are to be provided.

Example: For a retainer of $500 or more, the lawyer should at least prepare and file a complaint and have it served on the defendant (or defendants). What you want to avoid is a situation where you pay your lawyer a retainer, he or she writes a letter and makes a few phone calls to the defendant, then tells you the retainer is used up and more money is required to continue.

Working with the Lawyer

Once you have made a decision to hire the lawyer, and the lawyer agrees to take the case, be sure to let the lawyer know what kind of client you are. How involved do you want to be in the case? Do you want to be informed of each step in the case? Would you like copies of each document the lawyer files or receives in your case? Realize that you may be expected to pay for copies if there are costs involved. Alternatively, you may ask your lawyer to make the file available to you on a regular basis to view at his or her office to keep current with developments in your case.

Your lawyer should be able to take you through the case step-by-step to explain the procedures and anticipated timeline in your case. Ask the lawyer how often you can expect him or her to notify you about your case. If you know the general timeline of your case, it will help you understand how often to expect contact from the lawyer. For example, once your initial documents are filed, it may be at least 30 days (or longer) before the defendant files any documents in the case. Set up a method of contact that is convenient for you and reasonable for your lawyer. Many problems can be resolved by clear communications between the plaintiff and the lawyer.

GLOSSARY

A

accountability. The legal responsibility for a crime of a person who aids another in committing the crime. For example, the driver is just as accountable for a homicide in which he plans the crime with the passenger who actually shoots the victim.

acquittal. A "not guilty" decision. It is not the same as saying that the defendant is innocent. Instead, it says that the prosecutor did not prove the defendant's guilt beyond a reasonable doubt.

adjournment. A continuance which resets the case to a later time.

age of majority. The age at which a minor is treated as an adult, usually age 18.

alibi. A defense that can be raised to show that the defendant was not present at the time he or she is charged with committing the crime. The prosecutor must prove that the defendant was present.

alimony. Money paid to an ex-spouse on a regular basis after a divorce as ordered by the court.

allocution. The right of the defendant to speak on his own behalf.

alternative dispute resolution. Also called ADR, this is an alternative method of resolving a law suit. In ADR, the parties seek a mediator to hear their case and make a recommended settlement, which can then be presented in court and result in a resolution of the suit.

answer. In a civil suit, this is the defendant's response to the complaint. It is filed in writing in court.

appeal. The defendant has a right to appeal the judgment of conviction for a criminal offense to an appellate court. The appellate court examines the record, based on the issues raised by defendant, to determine if serious error occurred, or if a legal error occurred. Unlike a trial, no witnesses appear in an appeal, and the decision is usually given by a panel of judges after review of the records and consideration of the state and defendant's legal briefs and arguments.

arraignment. This is an initial court appearance in which the defendant is informed of the charges against him or her.

arrest. The seizure of a person by police.

arrest warrant. A court order authorizing police to arrest the suspect.

assault. Conduct by the defendant that threatens or places the victim in fear of receiving bodily harm.

B

bail. Bond money paid to a court, by or on behalf of a criminal defendant, to secure defendant's return for court. Bail can be paid by defendant, another or even a bond service. If defendant violates the conditions of his release, his bond can be forfeited and he can be ordered into custody pending trial.

bailiff. This person is a court official whose job it is to keep order in the courtroom and, where necessary, guard the defendant while in court.

bar association. A local, state or national organization of attorneys. These often provide referral opportunities for attorneys who are members.

battery. Conduct by a defendant that causes bodily harm to a victim.

bench trial. A trial held before a judge without a jury.

beyond a reasonable doubt. The standard of proof in a criminal case that the state must meet in order to obtain a conviction.

bill of rights acts. These are laws that give victims rights to obtain information and participate in their cases.

bond. Usually money or another thing of value which is deposited with the court to secure defendant's future appearance at court. The amount of the bond is set by a judge or magistrate. Defendant may have to pay all or a percentage of the bond amount. In some cases, bond is the defendant's signature that he will return. This type of bond may be called a personal recognizance bond.

boot camp/impact incarceration. A sentencing option, usually for non-violent offenders, in which the defendant must undergo an intensive training program. Most programs last for several weeks to months and are designed to permit a defendant to avoid a jail sentence.

burden of proof. The level of certainty of proven facts by credible evidence. The burden of proof is highest in a criminal case (beyond a reasonable doubt), and lower in a civil case (preponderance of the evidence).

C

cause of action. The theory or basis upon which a lawsuit may be filed.

circumstantial evidence. Indirect evidence that something happened. For example, if an offender has the victim's ring on his finder, it is indirect proof that he got it from the victim.

civil suit. A private suit between parties concerning personal wrongs, like personal injury cases.

clear and convincing evidence. The standard of proof that is greater than "preponderance of the evidence" used in civil cases, but less than "beyond a reasonable doubt" used in criminal cases. This standard is used in certain juvenile cases.

closing argument.   The final attorney's (or party's) argument in a case that sums up the evidence that party brought forth in the case and disagrees with, or distinguishes, the other party's evidence.

color of law.   An official who is acting in his or her capacity is considered to be acting "under color of law."

compensatory damages.   Recovery of out-of-pocket or tangible losses suffered.

complaint.   The document that begins a lawsuit and sets out the theory and claims of that suit.

concurrent sentence.   A criminal sentence that is served at the same time as another criminal sentence for a different crime.

confession.   A statement by a defendant, which may be oral or in writing, in which a defendant admits his guilt.

consecutive sentence.   A criminal sentence that must be served after the defendant has finished serving another criminal sentence for a different crime.

consent defense.   A defense that admits the acts, but claims that the victim agreed to the conduct.

contingent fee.   An attorney's fee that is due only if there is a recovery on the claim in the lawsuit. Thus, it is "contingent" on winning a judgment.

conviction.   The judgment entered by the judge that the defendant is guilty of the crime.

court of appeals.   A court which considers the case after the trial is completed to determine whether the law was applied properly. Many states have an intermediate level appellate court between its highest court (usually called the Supreme Court) and its trial court.

court reporter.   The person who records every word spoken in the course of proving a lawsuit.

crime mapping. The process of using computers in identifying where crime occurs in a community.

crime scene. This is the physical location of the crime.

crime victim's advocate. A person hired by the government or a private agency to assist victims negotiate the criminal justice process.

crime victim compensation. A right of recovery by the crime victim of certain out of pocket losses (such as funeral expenses) caused by the crime. Usually states require the victim to report the crime and cooperate with authorities in attempting to catch the criminal. The compensation comes out of a state fund. A victim usually has to make a claim within a short period of time after the crime to receive reimbursement of expenses.

criminal case. A case filed by the state against a defendant for a violation of a criminal law.

crisis intervention. A service offered to a victim within a short time after a crime to help the victim obtain needed assistance.

crisis lines. Also called hotlines, these are phone lines (and in rare cases Internet sites) that operate usually 24 hours a day and provide crisis intervention to victims or survivors of crime.

cross examination. Questions asked of a witness by the opposing party. For example, the victim may be cross examined by the defense attorney in a criminal case.

custody. The status of being held by law enforcement. For example, once a person is "arrested," he or she is in custody, which may continue after conviction until the end of the sentence of incarceration.

cybercrime. This involves crimes using or involving computers. Crimes committed using the Internet, for example, are called cybercrimes.

D

damages.   The financial, emotional or physical loss suffered by a person at the hands of another. Damages may be ordered to compensate loss or to punish the defendant.

defendant.   A person who has been charged with committing a crime.

deliberation.   The process by which a jury decides whether the facts proven in the case meet the elements required by law for a conviction.

delinquency.   A crime committed by a person under the age of 17. Juvenile delinquency cases are often prosecuted in special juvenile or family courts instead of criminal courts.

demonstrative evidence.   Graphics, charts or audiovisual aids which demonstrate a point being made by a witness at a hearing or trial.

deposition.   The taking of information related to the case from a witness under oath. Some states in criminal cases do not permit depositions of the victim, or provide for special limits on victim depositions.

direct evidence.   Eyewitness or some other direct evidence of a fact. For example, there is direct evidence of a robbery if a witness testifies that she saw the defendant steal the item from the victim.

direct examination.   Question asked of a witness by the party who called the witness to the stand.

discovery.   The process of providing information about a claim or defense. Discovery may be in writing, for example, as in interrogatories, or provided orally, as in depositions.

disposition.   A sentencing decision in a juvenile court.

DNA.   DNA stands for deoxyribonucleic acid, a genetic material that is compared with DNA collected from the victim, the crime scene or a defendant and analyzed to determine whether there is a match.

docket. The schedule of a court. This often refers to a court's daily caseload.

double jeopardy. The right to be free of a second prosecution for the same offense. With certain limits, one cannot be subjected to multiple prosecutions by the same jurisdiction for the same acts.

E

elements. The specific parts of a claim that must be proven. For example, in a criminal case, both a mental state and certain physical acts may be required as "elements" to be proven at trial beyond a reasonable double before a conviction can be entered.

entrapment. A defense in which the defendant claims that the state or government induced or encouraged him to commit a crime he otherwise would not have committed.

exhibits. The physical or tangible items introduced as evidence in court.

F

fabrication. A lie.

false imprisonment. The act of detaining a person without authority to do so.

felony. A sentence for a crime which subjects the defendant to one year or more incarceration.

felony review. Prosecutors who initially screen cases during preliminary investigation by police to determine whether it meets the legal definition of a felony offense.

forseeability. The reasonable belief that a consequence would follow an act. For example, one might say that it is forseeable that sitting in direct sunlight will produce a sunburn.

G

grand jury.   A group of jurors who consider a prosecutor's evidence and determine whether probable cause exists to prosecute a person for a felony.

H

half-way house.   A group or shared living facility that provides shelter to convicts who have been released from full custody incarceration or who have avoided prison.

harmless error.   An error which does not affect the outcome of the case. For example, on appeal, a court might find the admission of certain evidence to be in error, but if there was other strong evidence of guilt in the case, the court would likely find that the erroneously admitted evidence did not affect the outcome, therefore it was harmless.

hearsay.   An out of court statement which is offered in court to prove that it was true. Such a statement is generally not permitted, but there are many exceptions.

hung jury.   A jury is "hung" when it cannot reach a verdict in the case. This may result in a mistrial and the case may have to be retried. In rare cases, it will result in a dismissal of the case.

I

impeachment.   Questions asked by the other party which are designed to attack the believability of a witness.

incriminate.   A statement by a defendant that tends to show that he committed the crime.

indeterminate sentencing.   A sentencing structure that has no mandatory fixed minimum sentence.

indictment.   A formal charge of a felony issued by a grand jury.

indigent. A defendant (or litigant) is said to be indigent when he or she is without financial assets to be able to hire an attorney.

information. A criminal felony charge brought by a prosecutor.

injunction. A court order to do, or not to do, something. For example, the defendant may be enjoined in a civil case from withdrawing certain monies out of his pension plan or from hiding other assets, through an injunction.

in limine. A motion filed before trial to prevent evidence from being considered at trial. For example a defendant may file a motion in limine to prevent the state from using the fact that defendant was convicted of a similar crime in the past. The defendant will argue that such evidence will lead the jury to convict him because he is a "bad man,' not because he committed the crime for which he is on trial. There are exceptions which permit certain past criminal conduct to be admitted, so unless the parties agree, the judge will hold a hearing on the motion. Even if the judge excludes this evidence at trial, if the defendant is convicted, a prior conviction or prior criminal conduct will be considered in determining an appropriate sentence.

intent. The mental state which shows that defendant knew what he was doing and chose to continue to do so.

intentional infliction of emotional distress. A tort that seeks recovery for conduct intended to produce emotional pain and suffering for the plaintiff. This tort is seen where, for example, a parent watches the crime occur against his or her child.

interrogatories. Written questions, answered under oath, sent by one party to another in a lawsuit.

J

judgment. A final decision of the judge which resolved the case.

judgment proof. The state of having insufficient assets to pay any part of a judgment.

jurisdiction. The power of the court to decide a case before it. This usually turns on where the crime was committed, where the parties live or where the act occurred.

jury trial. The trial in which a jury decides the facts after hearing evidence and determines whether the party has proved its case. Jury trials take place in both criminal and civil cases.

juvenile. A person under the age of 17.

L

lesser included offense. A crime that has fewer than all the elements of a greater crime. For example, a "battery" (harmful physical assault) is usually a lesser included crime of "aggravated battery" (harmful physical assault with a deadly weapon).

lineup. A procedure in which the suspect is put into a group of similar individuals to see whether the witness can identify the suspect as the offender. If the victim is brought to the defendant (usually within a short time of the crime on the street), it is called a "showup."

M

malpractice. A practice of law that is less than acceptable or beneath the standard of reasonable attorney practices.

manslaughter. The act of killing another person while acting in a way that does not rise to the level of intentional conduct. This is sometimes seen in "heat of passion" cases.

miranda rights. The rights of a defendant which must be told to him by the police before he is questioned (taken from the case of Miranda v. Arizona). The rights include the right to remain silent, that anything the defendant says can be used against him in court and the right to have an attorney, which may be free if he does not have sufficient assets to hire one.

misdemeanor. A crime which usually carries a maximum jail time of one year or less (in a few jurisdictions, this is two years).

mistaken identity. The erroneous identification of a person as the offender for a crime.

mistrial. A ruling by the judge ending the trial, either due to serious error or when the jury cannot reach a verdict. A mistrial may end the case or the case may be retried, depending on the reason for the mistrial.

motion. A request to the court, seeking an order. Either party can file a motion before, during or after trial. The party that files the motion may be called the "movant."

mug book. A book maintained by police of the photographs of known or suspected criminals.

N

negligence. A failure to exercise care in the doing of, or the failing to do, an act.

no bill. A decision by a grand jury that the facts presented to it are not sufficient to indict.

no contest plea. This is a plea in which the defendant does not contest the state's facts. This may also be called a nolo contendere plea. The defendant is treated by a sentencing judge the same as if he was convicted through a guilty plea or after trial.

nolle prosequi. A decision by a prosecutor to dismiss the charges. It may be the end of the case or of the charges, but sometimes the charges can be refiled.

O

objection. A protest over a question that the attorney believes is improper. It is usually made before the witness answers the question. The judge then rules on the objection, either sustaining it (in which case the witness does not answer) or overruling it (in which case the witness must answer the question).

offer to settle. An offer by either party to end the case through a settled sum.

opening statement. An attorney's overview of the case, made just before the start of the testimony. The opening statement is not evidence in the case.

order. A judicial decision, usually made in writing.

P

pain and suffering. The intangible losses suffered by a victim of crime.

parole. The release from prison of a convict before the end of a felony sentence. There are usually special conditions of release, and while on release, the person paroled is under the supervision of a parole officer.

plaintiff. The person who originally filed a lawsuit.

plea. The defendant's response to a criminal charge (guilty, not guilty or nolo contendere).

plea agreement / plea bargain. To avoid a trial, the prosecutor and defendant may enter into a plea agreement in which the defendant pleads guilty or no-contest. The agreement may require the defendant to plead to some or all charges, and may make a specific sentencing recommendation. Plea agreements must be approved by the judge.

predator laws. Statutes that attempt to keep a known sex offender behind bars after he or she has served the original sentence due to the risk presented to the community.

preliminary examination / preliminary hearing. A hearing in which the Prosecutor demonstrates that there is probable cause to believe that a crime was committed and that defendant committed it.

preponderance of the evidence. A standard of proof that suggests that a fact more probably than not occurred. This standard is used in civil cases. It is a lesser standard than "clear and convicting" or "beyond a reasonable doubt."

pre-sentence investigation. A report prepared by a probation or parole officer after a defendant is convicted that gathers information about the defendant's prior criminal background, education, family, and social situation for presentation to the court at sentencing.

pre-trial conference. A meeting before trial in which the prosecutor and defendant may discuss plea bargains. A judge may participate in a felony pretrial conference.

probable cause. The reasonable belief, based on facts and circumstance presented, that a crime has been committed.

probation. A sentencing option for most misdemeanor and some felony convictions. This sentence allows the defendant to remain in the community under certain conditions and under the supervision of a probation officer.

process server. An official, usually a sheriff, or other court-appointed person who is charged with serving the complaint on a defendant.

pro per / pro se. A person who represents himself/herself in court without an attorney.

prosecutor. An elected or appointed official who is charged with the responsibility to enforce the criminal laws in court. Prosecutors may also be called district attorneys, state's attorneys, county attorneys, commonwealth's attorneys.

proximate cause. The act or conduct that is directly responsible for an injury.

punitive damages. The amount of money awarded to the plaintiff which is meant to punish the defendant for outrageous conduct.

Q

quash. To declare invalid. Defendant may ask that his arrest be quashed where he argues police did not have probable cause to arrest him.

R

rape. The act of forcibly engaging in sexual relations without the consent of the victim.

rape evidence collection kit. A standardized method of collecting evidence in a sexual assault case.

reasonable care. The responsibility to engage in due care for one's welfare.

reasonable doubt. A doubt based on the evidence produced at trial which questions whether a crime was committed or whether defendant committed it.

recognizance. A signature bond by which defendant obtains release from jail pending trial.

re-direct examination. The questions asked of a witness by their attorney (or the attorney who support their testimony) to correct any errors or misstatements made during the cross-examination.

relevant. Evidence which has a definite bearing on a fact to be proved in the case.

reparation, *see* restitution.

respondeat superior. The legal concept that holds an employer liable for the acts of its employees.

restitution. Payments ordered by the judge to repay victims for out of pocket property loss or injury expenses as the result of the crime. This is more limited than the potential for damages in a civil case.

retainer. The sum paid to an attorney to begin proceedings.

S

sale and levy.   The act of foreclosing on real property.

search and seizure.   The phrase is taken from the promise, in the Fourth Amendment to the U.S. Constitution, that says that persons have a right to be free of unreasonable searches and seizures of themselves and their property in a criminal case. A violation of this right may result in evidence being excluded from the case, and this may lead to a dismissal of the charges.

self defense.   The legal right to use force to protect yourself or another person, or property against some threat or harm attempted by another person.

sentence.   The punishment ordered after a conviction in a criminal case. A sentence may require payment of a fine, restitution or jail/prison time. Unless by a plea agreement, the sentence is entered after a hearing in which the judge (or in rare cases the jury) considers factors in aggravation (like the youth of the victim) or mitigation (like this is the defendant's first offense). Sentences for different crimes can be served consecutively or concurrently.

sentencing.   A determination of the punishment of a defendant made by a judge after a conviction is entered in a criminal case.

sequestration.   A method of protecting a juror (or witness) from outside influences. In rare cases, a jury may be sequestered during trial.

sex offender.   A person convicted of a sex crime.

sexual assault.   The act of forcibly engaging in sexual conduct with a victim. *See also* rape.

show up.   A limited, usually on the street, viewing of a suspect by the victim for purposes of identification.

small claims court.   A court that is limited in its jurisdiction to hearing cases in which the demanded recovery is less than a certain sum.

stare decisis. The rule that once a principle is decided it will be followed in future cases.

statute. Law passed by a legislature (as opposed to common law found in court decisions).

statute of limitations. Time limit within which criminal charges or civil lawsuits must be filed.

strict liability. The concept that a person (or a corporation or some other entity) will be held liable regardless of the intent of the person who does the act.

subpoena. A court order requiring a person to appear in court and give testimony as a witness, and/or to produce documents.

summons. A notice, sent by, or issues by, a court clerk, which requires the person's appearance in court.

supervision. A deferment of judgment in which a defendant must meet certain conditions. Used in minor cases, if the defendant is successful, the case is dismissed without judgment.

supreme court. Usually the highest appeals court in a state.

suspended sentence. A part of a jail/prison term which the defendant does not have to serve. Instead, he or she is put on probation and stays in the community under certain conditions.

T

testimony. The information provided by a witness on the stand in the courtroom.

theft. The conduct of taking an item of value from another with the intent to permanently deprive the other of their property.

tort. A private wrong. This is often the basis for a civil suit, such as an assault or negligence. This is the opposite of a criminal case which is a public wrong.

transcript.   The official record of the testimony given in a case.

trespass.   Entering or remaining on another's property without permission.

true bill.   An indictment issued by a grand jury that finds that the facts presented meet the requirements of the law for charging a crime.

V

venue.   The place (e.g., city or county) where a trial will be held.

verdict.   The finding of the judge or jury, as in "the jury's verdict was guilty."

victim-assistance program.   A program whose staff is dedicated to assisting the victim negotiate the criminal justice process. Staff will provide notice, information and often assist the victims in court.

victim impact statement.   The right of a victim to tell the court at sentencing the impact that the crime has had upon them and their family. Most states allow for a representative of the victim to provide such a statement, and some states allow family members to do so.

voir dire.   The questioning process by which a jury is selected. In some jurisdictions only the court questions the jury. In others, the attorneys may also ask questions.

W

warrant.   A court order authorizing an arrest (arrest warrant) or search (search warrant).

witness.   A person who testifies in court under oath.

wrongful death.   The tort designation used to sue for recovery of damages against a person who killed another. The plaintiff in a wrongful death case is usually a surviving family member.

APPENDIX A
VICTIM'S RESOURCES

Over the past few years, numerous public and nonprofit agencies that serve crime victims have developed websites and include a great deal of useful information on the Internet.

Federal agencies are particularly useful, since they include a considerable amount of resource information. Also, many of the websites below provide links to other sites that can be useful to victims. A listing of various agencies, their phone numbers, and website addresses follows.

Mothers Against Drunk Driving (private, nonprofit with over 500 chapters around the United States)

800-GET-MADD
http://www.madd.org/

National Center for Missing and Exploited Children (operates 24-hotline and is a national clearinghouse and resource center on abduction and sexual exploitation of children)

800-THE-LOST or
800-826-7653 (TDD)
http://www.missingkids.org/

National Center for Victims of Crime (nonprofit victims' rights and victim assistance organization; comprehensive source of crime victimization information and referrals to local victim assistance programs; and offers attorney referrals for civil suits

800 FYI-CALL
http://www.ncvc.org/

National Center on Elder Abuse (includes state by state listing of phone numbers to report elder abuse);

http://www.elderabusecenter.org/

National Child Abuse Hotline (Sponsored by ChildHelp USA, a nonprofit organization),

800-4-A-CHILD or
800-2-A-CHILD (TDD)
http://www.childhelpusa.org/child/hotline.htm

National Criminal Justice Reference Service (NCJRS) (extensive sources of information on criminal and juvenile justice; has a searchable database of federal information on victims)

800-851-3420
http://www.ncjrs.org

National Domestic Violence Hotline (Sponsored by the U.S. Department of Health and Human Services)(24 hour hotline)

800-799-SAFE (7233) or
800-787-3224 (TDD)
http://www.ojp.gov/vawo/newhotline.htm

See also National Coalition Against Domestic Violence

http://www.ncadv.org/index.htm

National Fraud Information Center (takes reports of telemarketing and Internet fraud and provides methods of avoiding fraud)

800-876-7060
http://www.fraud.org/

National Organization for Victim Assistance (oldest victims rights nonprofit)

800-TRY-NOVA (1-800-879-6682)
http://www.try-nova.org

OVCRC (Office for Victims of Crime) (has a resource center on victim information)

800-627-6872
http://www.ojp.usdoj.gov/ovc/

Parents of Murdered Children (provides support for parents and other survivors of homicide; provides local chapter referrals)

888-818-POMC

http://www.pomc.com/

EVERY STATE ALSO HAS INFORMATION ON THE INTERNET FOR CRIME VICTIMS SUCH AS VICTIM ASSISTANCE AGENCIES AND COMPENSATION PROGRAMS:

Alabama	http://www.agencies.state.al.us/crimevictims/
Alaska	http://www.dps.state.ak.us/vccb/htm/
Arizona	http://www.dps.state.az.us/voca/
Arkansas	http://www.ag.state.ar.us/
California	http://www.boc.cahwnet.gov/victims.htm
Colorado	http://cdpsweb.state.co.us/ovp/ovp.htm
Connecticut	http://www.jud.state.ct.us/
Delaware	http://www.state.de.us/cjc/index.html
Florida	http://legal.firn.edu/victims/index.html
Georgia	http://www.ganet.org/cjcc
Hawaii	http://www.cpja.ag.state.hi.us
Idaho	http://www2.state.id.us/iic/index.htm
Illinois	http://www.ag.state.il.us/
Indiana	http://www.state.in.us/cji/
Iowa	http://www.state.ia.us/government/ag/cva.html
Kansas	http://www.ink.org/public/ksag/contents/crime/cvcbrochure.htm
Louisiana	http://www.cole.state.la.us/cvr.htm
Maine	http://www.state.me.us/ag/victim.htm
Maryland	http://www.dpscs.state.md.us/cicb/
Mississippi	http://www.dfa.state.ms.us/
Missouri	http://www.dolir.state.mo.us/wc/dolir6f.htm
Montana	http://www.doj.state.mt.us/whoweare.htm
Nebraska	http://www.nol.org/home/crimecom/
New Hampshire	http://www.state.nh.us/nhdoj/index.html
New Jersey	http://www.state.nj.us/victims/
New Mexico	http://www.state.nm.us/cvrc/
New York	http://www.cvb.state.ny.us/
North Carolina	http://www.nccrimecontrol.org/vjs/
Ohio	http://www.ag.ohio.gov/crimevic/cvout.htm
Oklahoma	http://www.dac.state.ok.us/
Oregon	http://www.doj.state.or.us/CrimeV/welcome1.htm
Pennsylvania	http://www.pccd.state.pa.us/
Rhode Island	http://www.state.ri.us/treas/vcfund.htm

South Carolina	http://www.state.sc.us/governor/
South Dakota	http://www.state.sd.us/social/cvc/
Tennessee	http://www.treasury.state.tn.us/injury.htm
Texas	http://www.oag.state.tx.us/victims/victims.htm
Utah	http://www.crimevictim.state.ut.us/
Vermont	http://www.ccvs.state.vt.us/
Virginia	http://www.dcjs.state.va.us/victims/index.htm
Washington	http://www.wa.gov/lni/workcomp/cvc.htm
West Virginia	http://www.legis.state.wv.us/coc/victims/main.html
Wisconsin	http://www.doj.state.wi.us/cvs/cvc.htm
Wyoming	http://www.state.wy.us/~ag/victims/index.html

Appendix B
Legal Research

The victim's rights laws of every state differ, but all are found in the state statutes or codes, which are listed in Appendix B. To find your state's laws:

1. Contact your local police department for brochures or other information.

2. Contact your local prosecutor's office for copies of relevant laws, or speak to any available victim-witness personnel.

3. Check with your state attorney general's office for a victim's or crime bureau or division.

4. Do some legal research of your own.

"Paper" Research

Doing your own research means visiting a library. A large public library may carry legal/government books, but you may need to visit a law library in order to find updated copies of your state's legal statutes or codes. The actual title of the book is very important, so bring the relevant page from your state found in Appendix C.

Contact the closest appropriate library to determine hours and location. The reference librarians can help you find the set of books you need. Once you find the statute or code books, look for the section numbers listed in Appendix C for your state to find the exact laws. Some states have passed constitutional amendments for crime victims, which may be found in the

Constitutional volume of the same state statutes or code. Be sure to look for the most current supplement, as the laws are frequently changed.

Many victim's rights laws are found within a chapter or section of the state's criminal code. The criminal code will include the names, definitions, and elements of the various criminal offenses in your state. If you are interested in finding your specific crime and you don't have a statute or code citation, look in the index volume under the name of your crime (e.g., "assault and battery" or "aggravated assault"), or look in the index of the criminal code chapter or volume. The index will give you the statute or code section number.

Often, the statute or code books include case "annotations," which are summaries of various appellate court decisions that have interpreted and explained the laws.

The entire appellate court decisions are printed in state and regional "case reporters." These are sets of books that contain the full written opinions of the appellate courts. To find a case that is listed in the annotations, carefully copy down the case name and the numbers which follow exactly, or make a copy of the page with the case annotation on it. Next, find out where the case reporters are in the library. Many reporters have two or more "series" (i.e., instead of continuing to number the volumes, they started a second series which begins with volume 1). Also, there may be more than one reporter in which the same case can be found. Each state publishes a reporter of its cases, and there are also regional reporters which combine cases from several states in the same geographical area (as in the example below). Ask your reference librarian for assistance. The citation often looks as follows:

People v. Wheeler, 216 Ill. App.3d 609, 575 N.E.2d 1326 (1992)

Name of case	State case reporter citation		Regional reporter citation	Year published

Once you find the proper state or regional reporter, the case is found using the following method:

216	Ill. App.	3d	609
Volume	State Court	Series	Page Number

In this example, you would first locate the set of books marked "Illinois Appellate, Third Series." Then you would locate volume 216, and turn to page 609. On page 609 of volume 216 of Illinois Appellate 3d case reporter you would find the appellate court opinion in *People v. Wheeler*, decided in 1992. (This same case would also be found on page 1326 of volume 575 of the Northeastern Reporter, Second Series.)

If *People v. Wheeler* has been appealed to a higher state or federal court, there are other sets of books (called *Shepard's Citations*) that will lead you to the later case reporter citations.

"Online" Research

Online legal research has become more available in the past few years. Although there are expensive subscription services, today, there are numerous Internet-based sites from which some legal research may be done. Even if you are not "online," public libraries often make the Internet available to their patrons through the World Wide Web (a collection of home pages). This means that not only is online research a very fast method of finding the law, it is also affordable.

Legal news is available through the Internet. There is a great deal of information concerning businesses and corporations. Many courts have begun to put their cases on the Internet. For example, the United States Supreme Court puts its cases on the Internet within a few hours of their publication: **http://www.uscourts.gov**. Legislatures also put their laws and bills on the Internet:

http://www.thomas.gov

Searching the Internet is based on URLs (Uniform Resource Locators), also known as *addresses* or by using key words. Search engines for legal research include **http://www.Findlaw.com** and the Cornell Legal Institute at:

http://www.law.cornell.edu

Appendix C
State-by-State Laws

The State listings in this appendix are in alphabetical order, and give references for relevant victims' rights laws. The following information is given for each state:

THE LAW: This gives the official title of the set of books containing the state's statutes or code. It may also give other information that will help you locate particular sections of the law. Words in italics are the names of the publishers that are part of the title that appears on the volumes. Be sure to check for the latest updates of the statutes or code. These updates will either be found in a supplemental booklet inside the back cover of each volume, in a separate section of loose-leaf volumes, or in a separate supplemental book.

CRIME VICTIM COMPENSATION: This gives the citation to the particular statute or code section that deals with obtaining compensation from the state's crime victim compensation program. In addition to the statute or code, you may also want to see the book *Victims' Rights*, by William L. Ginsburg, which provides detailed information about applying for crime victim compensation from such programs.

VICTIMS' RIGHTS: This provides the citation to the particular statute of code section dealing with specific rights afforded to crime victims. It also gives a summary of those provisions.

STATUTES OF LIMITATION: This gives the citation to the particular statute or code sections relating to how much time a victim has in which to file a civil lawsuit against the offender or a third party, and gives a summary of these limitation periods.

Alabama

THE LAW: Code of Alabama

CRIME VICTIM COMPENSATION: Sections 15-23.1 to 15.23.23.

VICTIMS' RIGHTS: Sections 15-23-60 to 15-23-84 and Constitutional Amendment 557.
- Applies to felonies involving physical/personal injury, sex offenses, or family violence.
- Victim may designate a representative or court may appoint one for incapacitated victim; a parent may act as representative for child victim.
- Within 72 hours police must give the victim contact information, including name and phone number of prosecutor.
- Prosecutor may request that victim and immediate family members' residence, employment or other related information be kept private.
- Prosecutor must confer with victim prior to disposition of case.
- Victim has right to be present at trial, and may be seated at counsel table with prosecutor.
- Notice includes protection methods for intimidation; court must provide safe waiting area to minimize contact with defendant.
- Victim may present oral and written impact statement at sentencing and to parole board.
- Victim has right to notice of release, escape, or death of offender.

STATUTES OF LIMITATION:
Injury to person or sexual abuse discovery: Section 6-2-34.
Length of time: 6 years. (but see also Section 6-2-38, two year limitations period in some cases)

Alaska

THE LAW: Alaska Statutes

CRIME VICTIM COMPENSATION: Sections 18.67.010 to 18.67.180.

VICTIMS' RIGHTS: Sections 12.61.010 to 12.61.030; and Constitutional Amendment, Article 1, Section 24, Article II Section 24.
- Applies generally to all victims; additional rights for felonies and domestic violence.
- Victim impact statement can include opinion on restitution and recommendation of sentence.
- Restitution law (Section 12.55.045).
- Provides that addresses and telephone numbers of victims are confidential (12.61.110).

STATUTES OF LIMITATION:
Injury to person: Section 09.10.070.
Length of time: 2 years.
Sexual abuse: 09.10.060.
Length of time: 3 years.
Sexual abuse discovery: Section 09.10.140(b).
Length of time: More than 3 years after the plaintiff reaches the age of majority if it is brought under the following:
Conditions: (1) if the claim asserts that the defendant committed one act of sexual abuse on the plaintiff, the plaintiff must commence the action with 3 years after the plaintiff discovered or through use of reasonable diligence should have discovered that the act caused the injury or condition; (2) if the claim asserts that the defendant committed more than one act of sexual abuse on the plaintiff, the plaintiff shall commence the action within 3 years after the plaintiff discovered or through use of reasonable diligence should have discovered the effect of the injury or condition attributable to the series of acts; a claim based on an assertion of more than one act of sexual abuse is not limited to plaintiff's first discovery of the relationship between any one of those acts and the injury or condition, but may be based on plaintiff's discovery of the effect of the series of acts.

Arizona

THE LAW: Arizona Revised Statutes

CRIME VICTIM COMPENSATION: Section 41-2407.

VICTIMS' RIGHTS: Sections 13-4401 to 13-4437; and Constitutional Amendment, Article II, Section 2.1.
- Constitutional Amendment gives victim right to refuse interview, deposition, or other discovery request.
- Applies to felonies or misdemeanor involving physical injury, sex offenses, and juvenile cases.
- Victim may designate a representative; court may appoint one for incapacitated victim; parent may represent a child.
- Police must give the victim rights form, police report, contact numbers, and information on nearest crisis services.
- Within 7 days of filing charge, prosecutor must give victim notice of rights.
- Request notification of offender's release on bond, escape, and recapture.
- Right to be present at court proceedings; may request to confer with prosecutor.
- May present impact information and opinion on appropriate sentence at plea hearing; court will not accept plea unless prosecutor made efforts to consult with victim and victim had notice of hearing; restitution is mandatory.

STATUTES OF LIMITATION:
Injury to person: Section 12-541-42.
Length of time: 1 year.
Conditions: 2-years for assault and battery; 1-year for false imprisonment.

Arkansas

THE LAW: Arkansas Code of 1987 Annotated.

CRIME VICTIM COMPENSATION: Sections 16-90-701 to 16-90-719.

VICTIMS' RIGHTS: Section 16-21-106.
- Applies to all crimes and victims.
- Victim entitled to notice of scheduled hearings and continuances or changes of schedule.
- Prosecutors shall assist persons to obtain protection from intimidation.
- Notice of financial services, social services, and employer intercession where needed.
- Entitled to prompt return of property used as evidence.
- Victim has right to be present at trial and hearings (Evid. Rule 616).
- Court should, when possible, provide secure waiting area to minimize contact with defendant.
- Right to prepare and present a Victim Impact Statement (Section 16-97-103).

STATUTES OF LIMITATION
Injury to person: Section 16-56-104.
Length of time: 1 year. (assault and battery)

California

THE LAW: *West's* Annotated California Codes. These books are divided into sets of volumes according to subject, such as "Government Code," "Probate Code," etc., so be sure you have the correct subject volume.

CRIME VICTIM COMPENSATION: Government Code, Section 13959-13974.

VICTIMS' RIGHTS: Penal Code, Sections 679.01 to 679.04; and Constitutional Amendment, Article I, Section 28.
- Applies to felonies, misdemeanors, and juvenile cases.
- Parents may represent minor child, and next of kin may represent a deceased victim.
- Consideration of bail must include, as a primary consideration, protection of public.
- Victim may be present on same basis as defendant (Penal Code, Section 1102.6), and is entitled to a support person in court.
- Entitled to notice of scheduled hearings and charges, witness fees, civil claim information, and prompt return of property used as evidence.
- Prosecutor must notify victim of pretrial plea agreement before presentation to court.
- May request to make oral or written Victim Impact Statement at sentencing and parole consideration.
- Restitution is mandatory whether or not defendant receives probation (Government Code Section 13967); restitution order is enforceable as a civil judgment.
- Notice of release, escape, furlough, work release, or parole.
- Sexual assault victim has the right to a support person at a law enforcement interview.

STATUTES OF LIMITATION:
Injury to person: Civil Procedure Code, Section 340.
Length of time: 1 year.
Sexual abuse discovery: Civil Procedure Code, Section 340.1.
Length of time: 3 years after the date the plaintiff discovers or reasonably should have discovered that psychological injury or illness occurring after the age of majority was caused by the sexual abuse, which ever occurs later.
Conditions: (1) Every plaintiff 26 years of age or older at the time the action is filed must file certificates of merit as specified in by law; (2) Certificates of merit must be executed by the attorney for the plaintiff and by a licensed mental health practitioner selected by the plaintiff; (3) A complaint filed pursuant to (1 above) may not name the defendant or defendants until the court has reviewed the certificates of merit filed and has found, in camera (i.e., in a private hearing), based solely on those certificates of merit, that there is reasonable and meritorious cause for the filing of the action. At that time, the complaint may be amended to name the defendant or defendants.
Conviction of a felony: Civil Procedure Code, Section 340.3.
Length of time: 1 year after conviction.

Colorado

THE LAW: *West's* Colorado Revised Statutes Annotated.

CRIME VICTIM COMPENSATION: Sections 24-4.1-100.1 to 24-4.1-124.

VICTIMS' RIGHTS: Sections 24-4.1-301 to 24-4.1-304 and Constitutional Amendment, Article II, Section 16a.
* Notice of status of case.
* Information on victim services.
* Notice of hearings and schedule changes.
* Entitled to secure waiting area to minimize contact with defendant.
* Notice of final deposition.
* Notice of right to pursue civil judgment.
* Speedy disposition right.
* Right to provide victim impact information (Section 16-11-102).

STATUTES OF LIMITATION:
Injury to person: Section 13-80-103(1)(a).
Length of time: 1 year.
Sexual abuse discovery: Section 13-80-103.7(1) and Section 13-80-108(1).
Length of time: Within 6 years after a disability has been removed for a person under disability, or within 6 years after a cause of action accrues, whichever occurs later.
Conditions: Accrual is defined as the date when "both the injury and its cause are known or should have been known by the exercise of reasonable diligence."

Connecticut

THE LAW: Connecticut General Statutes Annotated.

CRIME VICTIM COMPENSATION: Sections 968.54.201 to 968.54.224 and Constitutional Amendment, Article 17.

VICTIMS' RIGHTS: Sections 54-222a to 54-233.
* Applies to persons who are physically injured as a result of crime.
* Police should provide victim with a card listing rights and refer victim to Office of Victim Services for assistance.
* May request information and to participate in case by informing Office of Victim Services.
* May request notice of status of case, bail decisions, plea bargain, and disposition.
* May request to be notified whenever defendant makes application to Board of Pardons or Parole, department of corrections, or sentencing judge for early release; victim to receive notice in writing, including date and place of any hearing.
* Victim has right to make oral or written impact statement.

STATUTES OF LIMITATION:
Injury to person: Section 52-577.
Length of time: 3 years
Sexual abuse discovery: Section 52-577d
Conditions: "Notwithstanding the provisions of section 52.577, no action to recover damages for personal injury to a minor, including emotional distress, caused by sexual abuse, sexual exploitation or sexual assault may be brought by such person later that 17 years from the date such person attains the age of majority."

Delaware

THE LAW: Delaware Code Annotated.

CRIME VICTIM COMPENSATION: Title 11, Section 9001.

VICTIMS' RIGHTS: Title 11, Sections 9401 to 9418.
- Police must give victim rights information upon contact with victim.
- Victim entitled to designate representative.
- Prosecutor must confer with victim prior to disposition of case.
- Victims are entitled to a safe waiting area which minimizes contact with defense.
- Victim entitled to be present during court proceedings on same basis as defendant.
- Disclosure of victim and family's name and address is prohibited without court order upon good cause shown.
- Victim entitled to notice of escape or release of defendant.
- Victim entitled to make impact statement prior to sentencing and parole decision, and to obtain notice of disposition.

STATUTES OF LIMITATION:
Injury to person: Title 10, Section 8119.
Length of time: 2 years.

District of Columbia

THE LAW: District of Columbia Code.

CRIME VICTIM COMPENSATION: Sections 3-421 to 3-436.

VICTIMS' RIGHTS: Section 23-103a.
- Applies only to assault, sodomy, kidnapping, manslaughter, murder, rape, robbery, aggravated assault, and other defined crimes.
- Representative may act for deceased victim.
- Victim has right to be present at trial, if it doesn't prejudice testimony.
- Entitled to write victim impact statement which will be made part of presentence investigation report for consideration by judge prior to sentencing.
- In victim impact statement, victim can express opinion on whether defendant should be paroled.
- Victim has right to address parole hearing board on whether defendant should receive parole.

STATUTES OF LIMITATION:
Injury to person: Section 12-301(8).
Length of time: 3 years.
Sexual abuse discovery: Section 12-301.
Length of time: Depending on claim 1-3 years after date of discovery.

Florida

THE LAW: Florida Statutes. These may be found in the official books published by the State, titled "Florida Statutes," or in "West's Florida Statutes Annotated." With "Florida Statutes" a new set of books is published in odd-numbered years, with supplements printed in even-numbered years. Also, new laws may be found in a set of volumes titled "Florida Session Laws."

CRIME VICTIM COMPENSATION: Florida Statutes, Sections 960.01 to 960.28.

VICTIMS' RIGHTS: Section 960.001 and Constitutional Amendment Art I, Section 16.
- Requires law enforcement to provide information on victim treatment, compensation, role of victim, and how to get information on protection from intimidation.
- Victims are entitled to notice of scheduled hearings and continuances.
- Provides for "civil restitution lien" (Section 960.29) imposed against real and personal property and future "windfall profits" of the defendant.
- Provides for civil enforcement (Section 960.29) of restitution lien for a period of 20 years.

STATUTES OF LIMITATION:
Injury to person: Section 95.11(3)(o).
Length of time: 4 years.
Sexual abuse discovery: Section 95.11(7).
Length of time: 4 years after discovery.

Georgia

THE LAW: Official Code of Georgia Annotated. **CAUTION:** This is not the same as the "Georgia Code," which is an outdated set of books.

CRIME VICTIM COMPENSATION: Sections 17-15-1 to 17-15-14.

VICTIMS' RIGHTS: Sections 17-17-1 to 17-17-15.
- Applies to defined "serious crimes."
- Permits victim to have a designated representative during disability.
- Requires law enforcement to give victim notice and information on victim rights, role of victim in criminal justice proceedings, crime victim compensation, and victim services.
- Entitled to notice of arrest, release, bail hearing, and decision regarding bail.
- Entitled to secure waiting area which minimizes contact with defendant during court proceedings.
- Prohibits transmitting to defendant victim's address, phone number, or place of employment (Section 27-3910).
- Permits victim to express opinion on disposition, and to file objection to parole.
- Restitution can be ordered as condition of parole (Section 17-14-4).

STATUTES OF LIMITATION:
Injury to person: Section 9-3-33.
Length of time: 2 years.
Sexual abuse discovery: Section 9-3-33.1
Length of time: 5 years of attaining age of majority.

Hawaii

THE LAW: Hawaii Revised Statutes. Ignore "Title" numbers.

CRIME VICTIM COMPENSATION: Hawaii Revised Statutes, Sections 351-1 to 351-52.

VICTIMS' RIGHTS: Sections 801D-1 to 801D-7.
- Applies to crimes and juvenile offenses; additional rights for victims of felony offenses.
- Must report crime within 3 months unless good cause present for delay.
- Entitled to notice of financial and social services available.
- Entitled to make written request for information about scheduling, changes, and final disposition.
- Victims of felony crimes entitled to receive notice of major case developments, including arrest, release, referral to prosecutor for charging, filing of charges, rejection, preliminary hearing date, grand jury date, trial, sentencing dates, and disposition.
- Entitled to secure waiting area while attending court proceedings; protection from harm or threat of harm as a result of cooperation with prosecution.
- Upon request, entitled to return of property within 10 days of its collection.
- Notice of escape, work-release, furlough, supervised release, parole, bail release, release pending appeal, and release at end of term of incarceration.

STATUTES OF LIMITATION:
Injury to person or sexual abuse discovery: Section 657-7.
Length of time: 2 years.
Time does not run when criminal case is pending: Section 657-23.

Idaho

THE LAW: Idaho Code.

CRIME VICTIM COMPENSATION: Sections 72-1001 to 72-1025.

VICTIMS' RIGHTS: Section 19-5306 and Constitutional Amendment, Article I, Section 22.
- Applies to felonies, misdemeanors with physical injuries, sex offenses, and juvenile cases.
- Prosecutor must consult with victim.
- Entitled to be present at all case proceedings.
- Written victim impact information to be included in presentence report and victim may present orally at sentencing hearing.
- Entitled to notice of disposition of case.
- Restitution is a priority for all victims (Section 19-5304).
- Victim to be notified of all parole hearings and has right to present oral or written impact statement.
- Entitled to information about escape or release of defendant.

STATUTES OF LIMITATION:
Injury to person: Section 5-219(5).
Length of time: 2 years.
Sexual abuse discovery: Section 6-1704.
Length of time: 5 years of the child's 18th birthday.

Illinois

THE LAW: ILLINOIS COMPILED STATUTES (ILCS)

CRIME VICTIM COMPENSATION: Chapter 740, Act 45, Section 45.1 to 45.20, Illinois Compiled Statutes.

VICTIMS' RIGHTS: Chapter 725, Act 120; and Constitutional Amendment: Article I, Section 8.1.
- Applies to violent crimes, sex offenses, misdemeanors involving bodily harm or death, certain traffic offenses, and juvenile cases.
- Notice of status of filing of charges, date, time, and place of bail.
- Entitled to information on financial and social services available.
- Employer intercession services.
- Right to a secure waiting area to minimize contact with defendant while at court proceedings.
- Right to have support person present in court.
- May request information on bail release, disposition, and appeal.
- May request to be consulted before plea offer, and nontechnical explanation of plea agreement.
- Written victim impact statement in addition to presentence investigation report, and may present at sentencing hearing.
- May request information on release, escape, transfer to mental health facility, or death of defendant.

STATUTES OF LIMITATION:
Injury to person: Section 735 ILCS 5/13-202.
Length of time: 2 years.
Sexual abuse discovery: Section 735 ILCS 5/13-202.2.
Length of time: Within two years of the date the person abused discovers or through the use of reasonable diligence should discover that the act of childhood sexual abuse occurred and that the injury was caused by the childhood sexual abuse, but in no event may an action for personal injury based on childhood sexual abuse be commenced more than 12 years after the date on which the person abused attains the age of 18 years.
Conditions: If the injury is caused by 2 or more acts of childhood sexual abuse that are part of a continuing series of acts of childhood sexual abuse by the same abuser, then the discovery period under subsection is computed from the date the person abused discovers or through the use of reasonable diligence should discover (i) that the last act of childhood sexual abuse in the continuing series occurred, and (ii) that the injury was caused by any act of childhood sexual abuse in the continuing series.

Indiana

THE LAW: *West's* Annotated Indiana Code.

CRIME VICTIM COMPENSATION: Sections 5-2-6.1-1 to 5-2-6.1-48.

VICTIMS' RIGHTS: Sections 35-40-1-1 to 35-40-13-5 and Constitutional Amendment (Nov. 96).
- Crime must be reported with 5 days unless good cause exists for delay.
- Victim must cooperate with law enforcement.
- In certain cases, victim may request diversion to victim-offender mediation program (VORP).
- Court may revoke bond if defendant threatens or harms victim.
- Right to be present at court unless court orders otherwise.
- Entitled to information on notice of all hearings and proceedings, and scheduling changes.
- Entitled to information on financial, social mental health, and legal services available to victims.
- May request restitution.
- Victim impact statement may be in person or by video or audio tape.

STATUTES OF LIMITATION:
Injury to person: Section 34-11-2-4.
Length of time: 2 years.

Iowa

THE LAW: Iowa Code Annotated.

CRIME VICTIM COMPENSATION: Sections 910.1 to 912.12; 915.80.

VICTIMS' RIGHTS: Sections 915.1 to 915.50.
- Applies to crimes and juvenile cases.
- Entitled to information on crime victim compensation.
- Police or corrections to notify victim of escape of defendant.
- County attorney required to notify victim of continuances.
- Victim impact information can be filed in writing for consideration in sentencing.
- Can submit victim impact and opinion to parole board, and has right to know disposition.
- Victim restitution request.
- Protection for identification of child victim.
- Child victim entitled to have a guardian ad litem.

STATUTES OF LIMITATION:
Injury to person: Section 614.1.
Length of time: 2 years.
Sexual abuse discovery: Section 614.8A
Length of time: 4 years.
Conditions: An action for damages for injury suffered as a result of sexual abuse which occurred when the injured person was a child, but not discovered until after the injured person is of the age of majority, must be brought within 4 years from the time of discovery by the injured party of both the injury and the casual relationship between the injury and the sexual abuse.

Kansas

THE LAW: Kansas Statutes Annotated. There are two publishers of Kansas Statutes Annotated, so you may find the volumes titled "Kansas Statutes Annotated, Official," or "Vernon's Kansas Statutes Annotated." Both sets have very poor indexes, and the numbering system can be confusing, so you may want to ask the librarian for assistance.

CRIME VICTIM COMPENSATION: Sections 74-7301 to 74-7320 and Constitutional Amendment Article 15, Section 15.

VICTIMS' RIGHTS: Sections 74-7333 to 74-7335.
- Applies to "serious crimes" defined in statute, and includes juveniles.
- Right to notice of all public hearings, including preliminary, trial, sentencing, and expungement.
- Statewide victim's rights hotline maintained by attorney general.

STATUTES OF LIMITATION:
Injury to person: Section 60.513, 60-514.
Length of time: 1 year or 2 years depending on claim.
Sexual abuse discovery: Section 60-523.
Length of time: 3 years after child turns 18.

Kentucky

THE LAW: Kentucky Revised Statutes.

CRIME VICTIM COMPENSATION: Sections 346.010 to 346.190.

VICTIMS' RIGHTS: Sections 421.500 to 421.576.
- Applies to persons who are victims of "serious crimes" as defined, including family violence.
- At initial contact, police will give notice of emergency services, (including social and medical), community treatment, and crime victim compensation available to victims.
- Police will explain methods of protection from intimidation, the criminal justice process, and provide information on arrest.
- Speedy trial in child sexual abuse cases.
- Entitled to prompt return of property and employer intercession.
- Prosecutor will consult with victim prior to dismissal, release, negotiating plea, or pretrial diversion disposition.
- On request, victim entitled to notice of hearings, release of defendant, filing of charges, and trial date.
- Victim entitled to make a victim impact statement and comment on sentence to be included in presentence investigation report for consideration at sentencing, and may request notification and present victim impact information at parole hearing.

STATUTES OF LIMITATION:
Injury to person: Section 413.140(1)(a).
Length of time: 1 year.
Childhood sexual abuse: Section 413.249
Length of time: 5 years after child turns 18 or date of discovery subject to certain conditions.

Louisiana

THE LAW: *West's* L.S.A. (for Louisiana Statutes Annotated). This set of books are divided into sets of volumes according to subject, such as "Revised Statutes," "Civil Code," "Criminal Procedure," etc., so be sure you have the correct set.

CRIME VICTIM COMPENSATION: Sections 46:1802 to 46:1821.

VICTIMS' RIGHTS: Sections 46.1841 to 46.1844.
- Applies to felonies, misdemeanors, and juvenile cases.
- Must report within 72 hours of the crime, except for good cause shown.
- Entitled to information on rights, including availability of crime victim compensation, treatment, counseling, role of victim, stages of criminal process, and protection from intimidation.
- On request, entitled to notice of arrest, bail release.
- Speedy trial right.
- Law enforcement must provide private interviewing rooms.
- Prosecutor must confer with victim prior to disposition and discuss sentencing alternatives.
- Victim impact statement for consideration in sentencing hearing by victim and family members.
- Restitution as a condition of probation or parole.
- Notification of escape or release of prisoner.

STATUTES OF LIMITATION:
Injury to person: Civil Code, Section 3492.
Length of time: 1 year.
Crime of violence: Article 3493.10.
Length of time: 2 years.
Abuse of minor: Article 3496.1.
Length of time: 3 years from age of majority.

Maine

THE LAW: Maine Revised Statutes Annotated.

CRIME VICTIM COMPENSATION: Title 5, Sections 3360 to 3360-M.

VICTIMS' RIGHTS: Title 15, Section 6101.
- Applies to serious crimes, sex offenses, and domestic violence.
- Prosecutor shall notify victim of victim compensation availability.
- Victim entitled to notice of plea agreement before it is entered into court.
- Notification of time and place of trial.
- Written victim impact information for consideration in sentencing, and oral presentation at hearing.
- Prosecutor must inform court of victim's position on plea or sentence.
- Restitution is mandatory (Title 17A, Sections 54.1322 to 54.1330).

STATUTES OF LIMITATION:
Injury to person: Title 14, Section 753.
Length of time: 2 years.
Injury to person or sexual abuse discovery: Title 14, Section 752-C.
Actions based on crime: Title 14, Section 752-E.
Length of time: 3 years of discovery of profits from crime.
Conditions: "Actions based upon sexual acts toward minors maybe commenced at any time."

Maryland

THE LAW: Annotated Code of Maryland. These books are arranged by subject, such as "Courts & Judicial Procedure," "Family Law," etc., so be sure you have the correct volume.

CRIME VICTIM COMPENSATION: Article 26.A; Section 1 - 18.

VICTIMS' RIGHTS: Article 27, Section 761 and Constitutional Amendment Article 47.
- Notice includes information on crime victim compensation and social services.
- Entitled to separate waiting area to minimize contact with defendant.
- On request, kept informed of scheduled hearing and continuances.
- Speedy trial right.
- Right to make a victim impact statement.
- May request restitution.
- Notice of parole hearing and release in advance; and escape or furlough.
- Presumption of restitution (Article 27, Section 640).
- Requires sale of property or wage deduction for unpaid restitution (Article 27, Section 806).

STATUTES OF LIMITATION:
Injury to person: Courts & Judicial Proceedings, Section 5-101.
Length of time: 3 years (1 year for assault, Section 5-105).

Massachusetts

THE LAW: Annotated Laws of Massachusetts.

CRIME VICTIM COMPENSATION: Chapter 258C, Sections 1 to 13.

VICTIMS' RIGHTS: Ch. 258B, Sections 1 to 13.
- Applies to crimes and juvenile cases.
- Entitled to protection from intimidation and methods.
- Entitled to secure waiting area to minimize contact with defendant during court appearance.
- Entitled to information from prosecutor on disposition, release of defendant, scheduling, and continuances.
- May request restitution.
- Entitled to information from prosecutor on disposition.

STATUTES OF LIMITATION:
Injury to person: Ch. 260, Section 4.
Length of time: 3 years.
Sexual abuse discovery: Chapter 260, Section 4C.
Length of time: 3 years after child turns 18 or discovery (under certain conditions).

Michigan

THE LAW: Michigan Compiled Laws Annotated (abbreviated "M.C.L.A."), or Michigan Statutes Annotated (abbreviated "M.S.A."). Michigan has sets of books by two separate publishers, each with its own numbering system. Both have a cross-reference index to the other set. The references below give the cites to both sets. Ignore the volume and "Chapter" numbers.

CRIME VICTIM COMPENSATION: Michigan Compiled Laws Annotated, Sections 18.351 to 18.368; Michigan Statutes Annotated, Section 3.372(1) to Section 3.372(18).

VICTIMS' RIGHTS: M.C.L.A. Section 780.751; M.S.A. Section 28.1287(751); and Constitutional Amendment: Article I Section 24.
- Applies to felony crimes and juvenile cases.
- Law enforcement must give written notice of rights, including phone number and address of police and prosecutor.
- On evidence of threat to victim, prosecutor can seek to revoke bail.
- 7 days after arraignment and 24 hours before preliminary hearing, prosecutor must give notice in writing of rights and procedures for protection from intimidation, and provide name and contact of assigned prosecutor.
- Victim entitled to safe waiting area while at court; entitled to be present on same basis as defendant.
- Prosecutor must consult with victim prior to disposition.
- Victim privacy for address or other private information.
- Restitution mandatory (M.C.L.A., Section 780.766; M.S.A., Section 28.1287).
- Oral or written victim impact statement prior to sentencing.
- Entitled to notice of escape or release.

STATUTES OF LIMITATION:
Injury to person: M.C.L.A., Section 600.5805(9); M.S.A., Section 27A-5805.
Length of time: 3 years.

Minnesota

THE LAW: Minnesota Statutes Annotated.

CRIME VICTIM COMPENSATION: Sections 611A.51 to 611A.68.

VICTIMS' RIGHTS: Sections 611A.03 to 611A.06, Section 611A.031
- Crimes, includes local ordinance violations if bodily harm to victim; juvenile & certain traffic offenses.
- Law enforcement must deliver notice of rights to victim.
- Can request law enforcement to withhold identity in public records.
- May not be compelled to state address of home or business in open court.
- Entitled to notice of plea agreement and input prior to pretrial diversion.
- Victim impact statement for consideration in sentencing.
- Restitution request (Section 611A.04).
- Notice of escape or release.

STATUTES OF LIMITATION:
Injury to person: Section 541.07(1).
Length of time: 2 years.
Injury to person or sexual abuse discovery: Section 541.073
Length of time: An action for personal injury caused by sexual abuse must be commenced within 6 years of the time the plaintiff knew or had reason to know the injury was caused by the sexual abuse.
Conditions: In a cause of action for damages commenced against a person who caused the plaintiff's personal injury either by (1) committing sexual abuse against the plaintiff, or (2) negligently permitting sexual abuse against the plaintiff to occur: The plaintiff need not establish which act in a continuous series of sexual abuse acts by the defendant caused the injury. The knowledge of a parent or guardian may not be imputed to a minor.

Mississippi

THE LAW: Mississippi Code 1972 Annotated.

CRIME VICTIM COMPENSATION: Sections 99-41-1 to 41-29.

VICTIMS' RIGHTS: Sections 99-36-5, 99-43-1 to 99-43-49, and Constitutional Amendment Article 14.
- Applies to all crimes and juvenile cases.
- Must report crime within 5 days to be eligible for rights, unless good cause shown.
- Police must notify of defendant's escape or release from jail.
- Same right as defendant to be present in court.
- Right to transcript of proceeding at own cost.
- Victim's identity maybe withheld upon petition based on threats or harm.
- Restitution request.

STATUTES OF LIMITATION:
Injury to person: Section 15-1-35.
Length of time: 1 year (3 years in certain cases, Section 15-1-49).

Missouri

THE LAW: *Vernon's* Annotated Missouri Statutes.

CRIME VICTIM COMPENSATION: Sections 595.010 to 595.075.

VICTIMS' RIGHTS: Sections 595.200 to 595.215 and Constitutional Amendment Article I, Section 32.
- Applies to dangerous crimes against persons; other crimes by request.
- Must report within 5 days or show good cause for excuse.
- Right to be informed of status of case.
- Right to notice of defendant's release on bond.
- Entitled to a secure waiting area which minimizes contact with defendant.
- Return of property within 5 days of request.
- Right to information on restitution [Section 595.209 (11)].
- Employer may not discipline victim or family member for honoring subpoena.

STATUTES OF LIMITATION:
Injury to person: Section 516.140.
Length of time: 2 years.
Sexual abuse discovery: Section 537.046.
Conditions: In any civil action for recovery of damages suffered as a result of childhood sexual abuse, the time for commencement of the action must be within 5 years of the date the plaintiff attains the age of 18, or within 3 years of the date the plaintiff discovers or reasonably should have discovered that the injury or illness was caused by child sexual abuse, whichever later occurs.

Montana

THE LAW: Montana Code Annotated. The code sections are in a set of black, soft-cover volumes. The annotations are in a separate set of loose-leaf binders.

CRIME VICTIM COMPENSATION: Montana Code Annotated, Sections 53-9-101 to 53-9-133.

VICTIMS' RIGHTS: Sections 46-24-101 to 46-24-213.
- Applies to felonies, misdemeanors with bodily harm, or the family of homicide victim.
- Attorney General required to provide a form for notice.
- Prosecution must consult on plea before disposition.
- Employer may not discharge or discipline victim or family for participation in case.
- Upon request, felony victim can submit a statement to parole board.
- Entitled to reasonable notice of release on furlough, work release, or community program.

STATUTES OF LIMITATION:
Injury to person or sexual abuse discovery: Section 27-2-204.
Length of time: 2 years (3 years under certain claims).
Sexual abuse discovery: Section 27-2-216.
Conditions: An action based on intentional conduct brought by a person for recovery of damages for injury suffered as a result of childhood sexual abuse must be commenced not later that: (a) 3 years after the act of childhood sexual abuse that is alleged to have caused the injury; or (b) 3 years after the plaintiff discovers or reasonably should have discovered that the injury was caused by the act of childhood sexual abuse.

Nebraska

THE LAW: Revised Statutes of Nebraska.

CRIME VICTIM COMPENSATION: Sections 81-1801 to 81-1842.

VICTIMS' RIGHTS: Sections 81-1843 to 81-1850.
- Applies to defined crimes and to family members of homicide victims.
- Entitled to a copy of police report, arrest warrant, and indictment.
- Entitled to information on status of case and hearings.
- Right to testify before parole board or submit statement.
- Right to notice of disposition.
- Entitled to notice of release, escape, or discharge.
- Victim name and identifying information is not public information.

STATUTES OF LIMITATION:
Injury to person: Section 25-208.
Length of time: 1 year (certain torts may be brought within 4 years, Section 25-207).

Nevada

THE LAW: Nevada Revised Statutes Annotated.

CRIME VICTIM COMPENSATION: Sections 217.010 to 217.270 and Constitutional Amendment Article I, Section 8.

VICTIMS' RIGHTS: Sections 178.569 to 178.5698.
- Applies to victims or certain relatives of victims.
- Police will investigate and take measures to protect victim from intimidation.
- Entitled to notice of hearings and schedule changes.
- Entitled to make one telephone call.
- On written request, entitled to notice in writing.
- Court will provide secure waiting area to minimize contact with defendant.
- Entitled to prompt return of property and witness fee information.
- Notice of release from custody, and disposition.
- Sex crimes victims entitled to support person in court.
- All victim's personal information collected is confidential.

STATUTES OF LIMITATION:
Injury to person: Section 11.190.
Length of time: 2 years.
Child sexual abuse discovery: Section 11.215.
Conditions: An action to recover damages for an injury to a person arising from the sexual abuse of the plaintiff which occurred when the plaintiff was less than 18 years of age must be commenced within 10 years after the plaintiff; (a) reaches 18 years of age; or (b) discovers or reasonably should have discovered that his injury was caused by the sexual abuse, whichever occurs later.

New Hampshire

THE LAW: New Hampshire Revised Statutes Annotated.

CRIME VICTIM COMPENSATION: Sections 21-M:8-f to 21-M: 8-I.

VICTIMS' RIGHTS: Section 21-M:8-k.
- Applies to victims of felonies, and immediate family members of a minor, incompetent, or homicide victim.
- Entitled to information about criminal justice process, victim assistance, social services, financial services, and crime victim compensation.
- Right to prompt return of property.
- Notice of proceedings and scheduling.
- Same right as defendant to attend court.
- Right to confer with prosecutor and be consulted regarding disposition, including plea bargain.
- Oral or written victim impact statement to be considered in sentencing or plea agreement.
- Notice of change in status, escape or release of prisoner, date of parole hearing, and oral or written victim impact statement; notice of disposition.
- Notice and right to attend appeal proceedings.

STATUTES OF LIMITATION:
Injury to person: Section 508:4.
Length of time: 3 years (includes discovery rule).

New Jersey

THE LAW: NJSA (for New Jersey Statutes Annotated).

CRIME VICTIM COMPENSATION: Sections 52:4B-1 to 52:4B-33.

VICTIMS' RIGHTS: Sections 52:4B-34 to 4B-38 and Constitutional Amendment Article I, ¶22.
- Applies to all personal injury or property crimes.
- Includes nearest relative of homicide victim.
- Entitled to at least one phone call.
- Notice of 24-hour hotline.
- Victim impact statement to prosecutor prior to decision of whether formal charges will be filed.
- In-person statement directly to judge concerning impact.
- Restitution request and information Section 52:4B-36.
- Entitled to parole consideration of victim impact.
- Notice of escape or release.

STATUTES OF LIMITATION:
Injury to person: Section 2A:14-2.
Length of time: 2 years.

New Mexico

THE LAW: New Mexico Statutes 1978 Annotated.

CRIME VICTIM COMPENSATION: Chapter 31, Article 22.

VICTIMS' RIGHTS: Section 31-26-1 to 31-26-14 and Constitutional Amendment: Article 2, Section 24.
- Applies to defined crimes (includes: arson, aggravated assault, aggravated battery, murder, voluntary and involuntary manslaughter, kidnapping, criminal sexual penetration, and criminal sexual contact of a minor, homicide, and great bodily harm by vehicle).
- Victim includes family representative where victim is minor, incompetent, or deceased.
- Must report crime within 5 days or have good cause; rights are effective upon filing charges.
- Police provide written contact and status notice, including name and phone number of prosecutor.
- May appoint a representative.
- 7 days after filing charge, prosecutor must provide victim with written rights.
- Right to be present at court proceedings.
- Right to notice of escape.

STATUTES OF LIMITATION:
Injury to person: Section 37-1-8.
Length of time: 3 years.

New York

THE LAW: McKinney's Consolidated Laws of New York Annotated. These books are divided into subjects, such as "Penal Law," "Domestic Relations Law," etc., so be sure you have the correctly titled volume.

CRIME VICTIM COMPENSATION: N.Y. Exec. Law Chapter 620.

VICTIMS' RIGHTS: N.Y. Exec. Law Chapter. 640 to 649.
- Applies to violent felonies, and property crimes over a certain amount.
- Police must interview victim privately.
- Police must provide sex crimes victims with notice of nearest rape crisis center.
- Entitled to secure waiting area to minimize contact with defendant during attendance at court proceedings.
- Entitled to provide victim impact information for consideration in sentencing.
- Right to restitution (Penal Law, Section 60.27).

STATUTES OF LIMITATION:
Injury to person: N.Y. CIV. PRAC. L. & R. Section 214.
Length of time: 3 years. (1 year for certain claims, Section 215).

North Carolina

THE LAW: General Statutes of North Carolina. Lawyers and judge commonly refer to these as the "North Carolina General Statutes," although that is not the title as printed on the cover of the volumes.

CRIME VICTIM COMPENSATION: North Carolina General Statutes, Sections 15B-1 to 15B-25.

VICTIMS' RIGHTS: Sections 15A-824 and 15A- 841 and Constitutional Amendment.
- Applies to serious misdemeanors, felonies, and juvenile cases; includes family members of homicide victim.
- Entitled to request prosecutor to object to questions regarding victim's home address.
- Entitled to information on protection from harm.
- Same right to be present in court as defendant.
- On request, entitled to make a victim impact statement for consideration in sentencing.
- May request information on escape or release of prisoner.
- Right to restitution.

STATUTES OF LIMITATION:
Injury to person: Section 1-52(5).
Length of time: 3 years. (1 year for certain claims, Section 1-54).

North Dakota

THE LAW: North Dakota Century Code Annotated.

CRIME VICTIM COMPENSATION: Sections 54-23.4-01 to 54-23.4-18.

VICTIMS' RIGHTS: Sections 12.1-34-.01 to 12.1-34-.05.
- Applies to felonies, specified misdemeanors, and juvenile cases.
- Right to be informed of status of investigation.
- Right to notice of charges filed, procedures followed, pretrial release and conditions, participation in court (advance notice), and continuances.
- Entitled to information on social services.
- Entitled to secure waiting area, prompt return of property.
- May not be compelled to testify as to address, phone number, or other personal information without court approval.
- Right to be present in court, subject to rules of evidence.
- Written victim impact statement; comment on sentence and restitution; oral statement at judge's discretion.
- Notice of disposition, release, escape, work-release, or community or mental health release; right to have impact statement presented in parole and pardon procedures.
- Right to provide impact statement to parole board, governor or pardon advisory board.

STATUTES OF LIMITATION:
Injury to person: Section 28-01-18.
Length of time: 2 years.

Ohio

THE LAW: *Page's* Ohio Revised Code Annotated. Look for the title number, which will be the same as the first two numbers of the section number listed below. For example, to find Section 3103.05, you would look for the volume marked "Title 31."

CRIME VICTIM COMPENSATION: Sections 2743.51 to 2743.72; 2743.121; 2743.191; and 2743.20.

VICTIMS' RIGHTS: Sections 2930.01 to 2930.19; and Constitution, Art I, Section 10a.
- Applies to any felony and other defined crimes.
- Victim may designate representative; court may appoint representative for minor, incapacitated, or deceased victim.
- Police must provide written information about rights, social, and financial services, and a contact number.
- Notice of arrest and release information; prosecutor can request revocation of bond if victim threatened or harmed.
- Notice of scheduled hearings; victim may object to delay; prosecutor must confer with victim before dismissing charge or entry of plea; victim entitled to name of case and case number.
- Right to be present in court, subject to rules of evidence; right to secure waiting area to minimize contact with defendant; victim may have support person present.
- Victim cannot be compelled to testify as to address, phone number, or similar identifying information if threat or harm present.
- Victim impact statement (written or oral) includes restitution and comment on sentence and release.
- Notice of incarceration, escape, release, death.
- Employer cannot discipline victim or family for participation in proceeding.

STATUTES OF LIMITATION:
Injury to person: Section 2305.11(a); Section 2305.10.
Length of time: 1 year or 2 years if bodily injury.

Oklahoma

THE LAW: Oklahoma Statutes Annotated.

CRIME VICTIM COMPENSATION: Title 21, Sections 142.1 to 142.18.

VICTIMS' RIGHTS: Title 19, Section 215.33 and Constitutional Amendment Art II, Section 34.
- Applies to violent crimes and juvenile cases.
- Includes family members of homicide victims, and witnesses to crime.
- Information on protection from harm and methods.
- Right to secure waiting area while attending court proceedings.
- Notice of financial and social services; employer intercession.
- Entitled to notice of scheduled hearings and continuances.
- Information on plea agreement.
- Victim impact statement for consideration by court in sentencing.
- Information about reversal of conviction.

STATUTES OF LIMITATION:
Injury to person: Title 12 Section 95(4).
Length of time: 1 year (2 years with certain conditions).
Sexual abuse discovery: Title 12 Section 95(6).
Length of time: 2 years or 2 years of discovery.

Oregon

THE LAW: Oregon Revised Statutes Annotated.

CRIME VICTIM COMPENSATION: Sections 147.005 to 147.365.

VICTIMS' RIGHTS: Sections 147.405 to 147.415 and Constitutional Amendment Article I.
- Declares victims are entitled to fair and impartial treatment.
- Victims are to be protected at each stage of proceedings.

STATUTES OF LIMITATION:
Injury to person : Title 12, Section 110.(12.110).
Length of time: 2 years.
Sexual abuse discovery: Title 12, Section 117 (12.117)
Length of time: 6 years after age of 18 (or 3 years from discovery under certain conditions).

Pennsylvania

THE LAW: *Purdon's* Pennsylvania Consolidated Statutes Annotated.

CRIME VICTIM COMPENSATION: Title 71, Sections 11.701 to 11.710.

VICTIMS' RIGHTS: Title 18, Sections 11.102 to 11.216.
- Applies to specified crimes; permits family member or advocate to accompany victim at proceedings.
- Specific criminal justice personnel are responsible to provide basic victim's information, including information on crime victim compensation, in writing within 24 hours of contact.
- Victim's address and phone number cannot be disseminated to other than police, prosecutor, and corrections without consent of victim.
- In personal injury crimes, notice of arrest by police and notice of escape from custody.
- In personal injury crimes, burglary, or certain vehicle crimes, the right to comment prior to the prosecutor's decision to reduce or drop a charge, or accept or change a plea.
- May make a victim impact statement to court for consideration in sentencing; right to restitution, if possible.
- May provide victim impact information for pardon or parole consideration.
- Entitled to information on release, individual work-release, furlough, community treatment, escape, or transfer to mental health facility.

STATUTES OF LIMITATION:
Injury to person: Title 42, Section 5524.
Length of time: 2 years.

Puerto Rico

THE LAW: Laws of Puerto Rico Annotated (L.P.R.A.)

CRIME VICTIM COMPENSATION: 25 L.P.R.A. 981

VICTIMS' RIGHTS: Internal Security: Title 25, Section 973
- Be treated compassionately.
- Free access to a telephone to communicate with his family or next of kin or with his legal counsel, as soon as he is in contact with the criminal justice system.
- Address and telephone numbers may be kept confidential when necessary for safety.
- Communications privilege for victim and his counsel.
- Right to protection from harm.
- Right to information on medical, psychological, social and financial assistance programs that are available in the Commonwealth of Puerto Rico.
- Be notified of the development of the investigation, proceedings and sentencing of the defendant.
- Be consulted prior to settling a complaint.
- Be present at all stages of the proceedings allowed by law.
- Entitled to separate waiting area.
- Right to make a victim impact statement to the court.
- Right to leave from employment to participate in criminal justice proceedings.
- Right to restitution.
- Right to return of property taken as evidence.
- Special procedures for minors and those with disabilities.
- Right to make victim impact statement at parole proceedings (Judiciary: Title 4, Section 1503a.).

STATUTES OF LIMITATION: 31 L.P.R.A. Sec. 5298

Rhode Island

THE LAW: General Laws of Rhode Island. Ignore "Title" and "Chapter" numbers.

CRIME VICTIM COMPENSATION: General Laws of Rhode Island, Sections 12-25-16 to 12-25-30.

VICTIMS' RIGHTS: Sections 12-28-1 to 12-28-12; and Constitution, Article I, Section 23.
- Victim must make "timely report" and cooperate with police.
- Police to notify victim of status at least every 3 months.
- Family member designated in death or incapacity of victim.
- Right to notice of arraignment and bail release, and court proceedings at which victim's presence is required; right to provide input at plea hearing.
- In misdemeanor cases, right to address court on impact and disposition at pretrial conference, at judge's discretion.
- Notice of available methods of protection from intimidation, and secure waiting area to minimize contact with defendant while at court.
- Notice of available intercession, witness fees, return of property, and financial and social services.
- In felony cases, right to address court on victim impact and sentencing, and victim impact for parole consideration; family member in homicide cases.
- Notice of disposition and release from incarceration.
- Right to request restitution; automatic judgement.
- Upon felony conviction, civil judgment automatically entered as to liability.

STATUTES OF LIMITATION:
Injury to person: Section 9-1-14.
Length of time: 3 years.
Childhood sexual abuse discovery: Section 9-1-51.
Length of time: 7 years (7 years after discovery with certain conditions).

South Carolina

THE LAW: Code of Laws of South Carolina.

CRIME VICTIM COMPENSATION: Code of Laws of South Carolina, Sections 16-3-1110 to 16-3-1350.

VICTIMS' RIGHTS: Sections 16-3-1510 to 16-3-1565.
- Applies to any victim who has physical, emotional, or financial harm as a result of crime.
- Young, elderly, or handicapped victim entitled to special consideration and attention.
- Entitled to freedom from intimidation and secure waiting area while at court; police to provide transportation to court and physical protection in courthouse; employer may not retaliate for responding to a subpoena.
- Information about financial and social services, witness fee, crime victim compensation availability, and civil remedies including lien on profits.
- Notice of release on bail and recommendations made, procedures, hearings, and continuances in time to attend.
- Right to attend court (subject to judge's discretion); right to have counsel represent victim in cases involving victim's reputation.
- Entitled to confer with prosecutor and plea information.
- Right to present written or oral victim impact statement to judge for consideration in sentencing; restitution is mandatory (Section 17-25-322).
- Notice of disposition and release from incarceration.

STATUTES OF LIMITATION:
Injury to person: Section 15-3-550.
Length of time: 2 years. (3 years if under 15-3-530).

South Dakota

THE LAW: South Dakota Codified Laws.

CRIME VICTIM COMPENSATION: Sections 23A-28B-1 to 23A-28B-44.

VICTIMS' RIGHTS: Sections 23A-28C-1 to 23A-28C-6.
- Applies to crimes of violence, certain vehicular crimes, and domestic violence.
- Family member designated as representative for deceased victim.
- Victim must notify prosecutor to participate and provide address; entitled to name of prosecutor assigned to case and right to be prepared as a witness.
- Notice of scheduled bail hearings, release, and right to testify on danger (Section 23A28C-1(3)).
- Notice of charges and elements, and dates of preliminary hearing and trial.
- Information on protection from intimidation.
- Right to be present in court, subject to judge's discretion.
- Victim input in plea negotiation and impact information (oral or written) as well as comment on appropriate sentence to court; written impact information for consideration in parole or commutation.
- Restitution may be requested in sentence of probation or incarceration.
- Notice of disposition and release from incarceration.

STATUTES OF LIMITATION:
Injury to person: Section 15-2-15.
Length of time: 2 years.
Sexual abuse discovery: Section 26-10-25.
Conditions: Any civil action based on intentional conduct brought by any person for recovery of damages for injury suffered as a result of childhood sexual abuse must be commenced within 3 years of the act alleged to have caused the injury or condition, or 3 years of the time the victim discovered or reasonably should have discovered that the injury or condition was caused by the act, whichever period expires later.

Tennessee

THE LAW: Tennessee Code Annotated.

CRIME VICTIM COMPENSATION: Sections 29-13-101 to 29-13-118.

VICTIMS' RIGHTS: Sections 40-38-101 to 40-38-302 and Constitutional Amendment Article I, Section 35.
- Applies to all crimes.
- Information on procedures and stages of criminal justice process.
- Priority scheduling of crimes against person.
- Information on recovery of property and crime victim compensation.
- In cases of violent crime involving death or serious injury, notice of bail release; in other cases, may request information.
- Notice of time, date, and location of hearings; and continuances.
- Information on plea negotiations and agreements; in cases of violent crime involving death or serious injury, right to give impact statement to court and to speak at parole hearings.
- In cases of felony involving death or injury to victim, victim impact statement becomes part of pre-sentence investigation report.
- Information on release, appeals process, restitution rights, and civil process rights.

STATUTES OF LIMITATION:
Injury to person: Section 28-3-104.
Length of time: 1 year.

Texas

THE LAW: *Vernon's* Texas Codes Annotated. These books are divided into subjects, such as "Civil Practice & Remedies," "Family," "Probate," etc., so be sure you have the correctly titled volume.

CRIME VICTIM COMPENSATION: Code of Criminal Procedure, Sections 56.31 to 56.61.

VICTIMS' RIGHTS: Sections 56.01 to 56.12; and Constitution, Article I, Section 30.
- Applies to crimes involving bodily injury or death; includes sexual assault, kidnapping, and aggravated robbery.
- Victim includes guardian or close relative of deceased.
- Right to adequate protection from harm and threats.
- At initial contact, police to provide written information on proceedings, bail, pleas, restitution available, appeal, and crime victim compensation.
- Consideration of bail must include safety of victim.
- Within 10 days of filing charges, prosecutor to provide notice of rights to victim, including right to request notice of time, date, location of hearings and continuances.
- Entitled to secure waiting area while attending court, prompt return of property, and employer intercession.
- Right to be present in court, subject to judge's discretion.
- Entitled to make victim impact statement to probation office for inclusion in presentence investigative report; notice of escape or release of defendant.
- Notice of parole procedures.
- Phone number of victim is not a public record and address may be kept confidential unless the scene of the crime.

STATUTES OF LIMITATION:
Injury to person: Civil Practice & Remedies, Section 16.003.
Length of time: 2 years.
Sexual assault: Civil Practice & Remedies Section 16.0045.
Length of time: 5 years (tolled if defendant is unknown by filing a suit).

Utah

THE LAW: Utah Code Annotated.

CRIME VICTIM COMPENSATION: Sections 63-25a-401 to 63-25a-428.

VICTIMS' RIGHTS: Sections 77-38-1 to 77-38-14; and Constitution, Article I, Section 28.
- Applies to felony crimes, certain misdemeanors, and juvenile cases.
- Permits designation of representative for victim.
- Within 7 days of filing felony, prosecutor must provide initial notice (oral and written) about electing to receive further notices, including notice of "important court hearings."
- Subject to rules of evidence, victim has right to be present at important court hearings and to be heard at defendant's initial appearance on issues related to release.
- Victim's address, telephone number and victim impact statement are not public records, and victim may not be compelled to testify to address, telephone number, place of employment or other locating information unless the victim specifically consents or court finds a compelling need exists to disclose the information
- Court must consider victim's interests in continuances.
- Can exercise victim impact statement through oral, written, audiotape, or videotape, to be included in presentence investigative report; where number of victims exceeds 5, court may limit oral statements to a representative number of victims.
- Board of pardons and parole must provide notice of parole procedures and hearings.

STATUTES OF LIMITATION:
Injury to person or sexual abuse discovery: Section 78-12-28.
Length of time: 2 years.
Sexual abuse discovery: Section 78-12-25.1.
Conditions: (1) A person must file a civil action for intentional or negligent sexual abuse suffered as a child: (a) within 4 years after the person attains the age of 18 years; or (b) if a person discovers sexual abuse only after attaining the age of 18 years, that person may bring a civil action for such sexual abuse within 4 years after discovery of the sexual abuse, whichever period expires later. (2) The victim need not establish which act in a series of continuing sexual abuse incidents caused the injury complained of. (3) The knowledge of a custodial parent or guardian shall not be imputed to a person under the age of 18 years.

Vermont

THE LAW: Vermont Statutes Annotated. Ignore "Chapter" numbers.

CRIME VICTIM COMPENSATION: Title 13, Sections 5351 to 5358.

VICTIMS' RIGHTS: Title 1, Sections 5301 to 5321.
- Applies to crimes involving injury or death, including juvenile cases.
- Victim includes family of deceased, minor, or incompetent victim; also applies to "affected persons."
- Crime must be reported to law enforcement; notice of bail hearing and input on bail decision.
- Information on level of protection available, witness fees, and restitution available.
- Entitled to short-term counseling, and referrals.
- Notice of financial, social services, prompt return of property, and employer may not discipline victim or family for responding to subpoena.
- Entitled to transportation to and from court where necessary.
- Except in juvenile cases, entitled to timely notice of hearings, continuances, final disposition, release and escape, and release on bail; right to be present at court proceedings.
- Right to provide victim impact statement at sentencing.
- Address and employment of victim protected unless it would prejudice defendant.

STATUTES OF LIMITATION:
Injury to person: Title 12, Section 512.
Length of time: 3 years.
Sexual abuse discovery: Title 12, Section 522 (1991) & Title 12, Section 560

Conditions: A civil action brought by any person for recovery of damages for injury suffered as a result of childhood sexual abuse must be commenced within 6 years of the act alleged to have caused the injury or condition, or within 6 years of the time the victim discovered that the injury or condition was caused by that act, whichever period expires later. The victim need not establish which act in a series of continuing sexual abuse or exploitation incidents caused the injury. If a complaint is filed alleging an act of childhood sexual abuse which occurred more than 6 years prior to the date the action is commenced, the complaint must immediately be sealed by the clerk of the court. The complaint must remain sealed until the answer is served or, if the defendant files a motion to dismiss under Rule 12(b) of the Vermont Rules of Civil Procedures, until the court rules on that motion. If the complaint is dismissed, the complaint and any related papers or pleadings will remain sealed. Any hearing held in connection with the motion to dismiss must be in camera (in private, usually in the judge's chambers). Related statute: When a person entitled to bring an action for damages as a result of childhood sexual abuse is unable to commence the action as a direct result of the damages caused by the sexual abuse, the period during which the person is incapacitated will not be taken as a part of the time limited for commencement of the lawsuit.

Virginia

THE LAW: Code of Virginia 1950. Ignore "Chapter" numbers.

CRIME VICTIM COMPENSATION: Sections 19.2-368.1 to 19.2-368.18.

VICTIMS' RIGHTS: Sections 19.2-11.01 to 19.2-11.04, 19.2-299.1 and Constitutional Amendment Article I, Section 8-A.
- Applies to all persons suffering harm as a result of felony or other defined crimes (includes assault and battery).
- Information about social and financial services, crime victim compensation, return of property, employer intercession, and right to interpreter.
- Notice of judicial proceedings and continuances.
- Information on intimidation and protection available; right to separate waiting area to minimize contact with defendant; right to special court procedures for certain sexual offenses.
- Victim's address, phone number, or similar private information is confidential unless the court orders otherwise; right to request law enforcement not to disclose address, phone or place of employment of victim.
- Written victim impact statement, to present to court (subject to rules of evidence) for consideration in sentencing. which may be presented orally.
- Notice of escape or release of prisoner.

STATUTES OF LIMITATION:
Injury to person: Section 8.01-243(a).
Length of time: 2 years.
Sexual abuse discovery: Section 8.01-249(6).
Conditions: In actions for injury to the person resulting from sexual abuse occurring during the infancy or incompetency of the person (whatever the theory of recovery), when the fact of the injury and its casual connection to the sexual abuse is first communicated to the person by licensed physician, psychologist, or clinical psychologist. However, no such action may be brought more than 10 years after the later of (i) the last act by the same perpetrator which was part of a common scheme of plan of abuse, or (ii) removal of the disability of infancy or incompetency.

Washington

THE LAW: *West's* Revised Code of Washington Annotated.

CRIME VICTIM COMPENSATION: Sections 7.68.070 to 7.68.340.

VICTIMS' RIGHTS: Sections 7.69.010 to 769A.050; and Constitution, Article II, Section 35.
- Applies to felonies and misdemeanors.
- Sexual crime or violent crime victims receive written statement of rights upon reporting crime, with crime victim/witness program information.
- Sexual or violent crime victims entitled to have crime victim advocate present at interviews.
- Information about return of property, final disposition and witness fees, employer intercession, and victim assistance.
- Notice of hearings and continuances including time, date, and location of trial and sentencing, and right to be present in court.
- Right to protection from harm or threats; safe waiting area to minimize defendant contact.
- Victim impact statement (written) included in presentence investigative report; oral presentation at sentencing hearing; in person, audio or videotape of impact statement at pardon or hearing on commutation of sentence.
- Restitution is mandatory, unless court orders otherwise [Section 7.69.030(15)].
- Special procedures for child victims.

STATUTES OF LIMITATION:
Injury to person: Sections 4.16.100, 4.16.080.
Length of time: 2 years or 3 years depending on claim.
Sexual abuse: Section 4.16.340.
Length of time: 3 years after age 18 or discovery in certain cases.

Conditions: All claims or causes of action based on intentional conduct brought by any person for recovery of damages for injury suffered as a result of childhood sexual abuse must be commenced within the later of the following periods: (a) within 3 years of the act alleged to have caused the injury or condition; (b) within 3 years of the time the victim discovered or reasonably should have discovered that the injury or condition was caused by said act; or (c) within 3 years of the time the victim discovered that the act caused the injury for which the claim is brought; provided, that the time limit for commencement of an action is tolled for a child until the child reaches the age of 18 years.

West Virginia

THE LAW: West Virginia Code.

CRIME VICTIM COMPENSATION: West Virginia Code, Sections 14-2A-1 to 14-2A-29.

VICTIMS' RIGHTS: Sections 61-11A-1 to 61-11A-8.
- Applies to any felony.
- Victim includes family representative for deceased victim.
- Police to provide information about rights, role of victim and procedures, and crisis, social, and financial services.
- Prosecutor to provide steps available for intimidation protection.
- Notice of arrest, initial appearance, release on bail, hearings and scheduling changes, entry of plea, trial, and sentencing.
- Prosecutor must consult victim of a serious crime regarding disposition of case, release on bail, and plea, diversion program.
- In cases involving injury to victim, impact statement (written) must be included in presentence investigative report; in child victim cases, recommendations on effect of disposition on victim; oral victim impact to court for consideration in sentencing.
- Notice of escape or release of prisoner.
- Restitution is mandatory (Section 61-11A-4), and may be enforced by state or by victim as a civil judgment.

STATUTES OF LIMITATION:
Injury to person: Section 55-2-12.
Length of time: 2 years.

Wisconsin

THE LAW: *West's* Wisconsin Statutes Annotated. Ignore "Chapter" numbers.

CRIME VICTIM COMPENSATION: Sections 949.001 to 949.18.

VICTIMS' RIGHTS: Sections 950.01 to 950.08; and Constitution, Article I, Section 9m.
- Applies to crimes and juvenile cases.
- Victim includes family of homicide victim.
- Crime must be reported to authorities who shall within 24 hours provide victim with notice of rights.
- Information about rights, social and financial services, witness fees, and employer intercession.
- Notice of bail release information in felony cases.
- Notice of hearings, continuances, and final disposition; right to have interest considered for continuances.
- Entitled to protection from harm and threats; right to secure waiting area to minimize contact with defendant.
- Victim impact statement and input into parole decisions.
- Notice of community release or parole; notice of pardon application to governor.
- Special procedures for child victims.

STATUTES OF LIMITATION:
Injury to person: Section 893.54.
Length of time: 3 years. (Section 893.57, 2 years for intentional tort claims).
Incest: Section 893.587.
Length of time: 2 years of discovery.
Sexual abuse by therapist: Section 893.585.
Length of time: 3 years after claim accrues.

Wyoming

THE LAW: Wyoming Statutes Annotated.

CRIME VICTIM COMPENSATION: Sections 1-40-101 to 1-40-119.

VICTIMS' RIGHTS: Section 1-40-201 to 1-40-210.
- Applies to all crimes.
- Police provide information about rights, social and financial services, interpreter/translator, return of property, employer intercession, and a contact number of officer assigned to case.
- Information on right to be free from intimidation and secure waiting area to minimize contact with defendant; right to have interest considered for continuances.
- Notice of status of investigation and release of defendant.
- Entitled to name and phone number of prosecutor assigned to case.
- Notice of scheduled hearings, disposition, sentencing, imprisonment, and release.
- Victims protected from discharge by employer due to involvement with court proceedings, including response to subpoenas.
- Same right as defendant to be present in court and to participate.
- Victim impact statement (written) included in presentence report and oral victim impact statement presented at sentence hearing.
- Notice of escape, release, or parole conditions.

STATUTES OF LIMITATION:
Injury to person: Section 1-3-105.
Length of time: 1 year to 4 years depending on claim.
Sexual abuse: Section 1-3-105(b).
Length of time: 8 years after age 18 or 3 years after discovery.

Appendix D
Sample Forms

This appendix includes sample forms. Use these as a guide when filling out of writing the forms that are applicable in your state and municipality.

Form A. Request Letter to Police

NOTE: *Write this letter to the officer in charge of your case. If you do not know which officer to address your request to, then send it to the police department in care of the police chief.*

[Your Name]
[Your Street Address]
[Your City, State, Zip Code]

[Date]

Re: **[identify your case, include police report number if you have one, or date of crime if not]**

Dear   **[Name or individual if known, if not address to "Investigator," "Detective," "Chief," etc.]**

I was the victim of a **[type of crime]** on **[date]**. Under the victim's rights law of this state, I am hereby requesting that you keep me informed as to the status of the investigation. Please provide me with the name and contact number for the officer assigned to my case.

Please contact me to confirm that you have received this letter. **[Give contact information here: e.g., "I can be contacted in the daytime at 555-9999 or 123 South Street, Apt. 202"]**. I look forward to hearing from you.

                             Thank you,

                             [Your signature]
                             [Your name typed or printed]

Form B. Request for Information from Prosecutor

NOTE: *Write this letter to the prosecutor in charge of your case. If you do not know which prosecutor to address your request to, then send it to the office of the prosecutor (sometimes called district attorney or state's attorney or county attorney).*

[Your Name]
[Your Street Address]
[Your City, State, Zip Code]

[Date]

Re: *[Identify your case, including police report number if you have one, or date of crime if not]*

Dear *[Name of prosecutor if known, or "Prosecuting Attorney"]*:

I was the victim of a *[type of crime]* on *[date]*. I hereby request a copy of the victim's rights laws of our state. I also request that you keep me informed as to the following: *[arrest, filing of charges, bail release of defendant, advance notice of hearings, and continuances, an opportunity to confer with you before you make a plea agreement]*. Finally, please provide the name of the attorney responsible for prosecuting my case and a contact number.

I look forward to prosecuting my case. Please contact me to confirm that you have received this letter. *[Give contact information here, e.g., "I can be contacted in the daytime at 555-9999 or 123 South Street, Apt. 202"]*. I look forward to hearing from you.

Thank you,

[Your signature]
[Your name typed or printed]

Form C. Request for Prisoner Information

NOTE : *Once the offender is incarcerated, write this letter to the department of corrections or prisoner review/parole board/county sheriff/juvenile detention center or mental health facility. If you do not know which department to address your request to, then contact your prosecuting attorney for information.*

[Your Name]
[Your Street Address]
[Your City, State, Zip Code]

[Date]

Re: *[Identify your case, including court docket number if you have one]*

Dear *["Warden," "Parole Board," "Review Board," etc.]*:

I was the victim of *[type of crime]*. The offender's name is *[name of prisoner]*. The date of conviction is *[date]*. Under the crime victim's rights laws of this state, I request that you keep me informed as to status of the prisoner in advance if possible, including: escape and recapture, release for work or furlough purposes, community release or transfer to a mental health facility, and final release date. Finally, please provide the date, time and location of any parole, pardon or commutation procedures which may be scheduled in this case. In addition, I would like to know the name and contact number of the probation or parole officer assigned to the case.

Please contact me to confirm that you have received this letter. *[give contact information here, eg., I can be contacted in the daytime at 555-9999 or 123 South Street, Apt. 202"]*. I look forward to hearing from you.

Thank you,

[Your signature]
[Your name typed or printed]

Form D. Victim Impact Statement

NOTE : *This statement is to be considered prior to sentencing the offender. Therefore it should be completed as soon as possible after the charges have been filed. Check with your prosecutor to see if they have a form for you to follow or use the one below.*

Victim Impact Statement

CASE: State v. <u>John Smith</u> [name of offender]
DOCKET/CASE NUMBER: <u>2001 CR 1009</u>
CRIME [list crimes here]:
<u>attempt armed robbery</u>
<u>aggravated vehicular hijacking</u>

Victim Information:

NAME <u>Rhonda Jones</u> AGE <u>46</u> PHONE <u>omitted</u>
ADDRESS <u>omitted</u> CITY_____
STATE_____
WORK ADDRESS <u>omitted</u> CITY_____
STATE____

I WAS THE VICTIM OF: [describe crime]
<u>The above crimes committed by the defendant on June 10, 2000</u>
<u>when defendant attempted to rob me at gunpoint, then threw me</u>
<u>out of the car and stole my 1997 Corsica, leaving me sprawled</u>
<u>on the street .</u>

Loss Suffered
[complete sections which apply to your case; attach documentation where possible]

I WAS PHYSICALLY INJURED: [include description of medical care or emergency treatment, hospitalization; list all doctors and hospitals; explain doctor's treatment, therapy, etc; Anticipated future physical impairment based on medical evaluation or doctor's statement]
<u>I was taken by ambulance to Janesville Hospital where I was</u>
<u>treated for a fractured hip, numerous bruises and contusions,</u>
<u>and received 4 stitches in my head. My bills thus far total</u>
<u>$7,500.and I continue to undergo therapy for my hip which is</u>
<u>anticipated to last another 9 months at an estimated cost of</u>
<u>another $2,500. Medication has also cost another $500.00.</u>

AMOUNT OF MEDICAL EXPENSES:

$ __7,000.00__ (TO DATE _of sentence_) (insert date of sentence)

$ __10,000.00__ (ANTICIPATED)

I WAS PSYCHOLOGICALLY INJURED: [include description of psychiatric or psychological care or treatment, hospitalization; explain doctor's treatment, counseling, therapy, etc; Anticipated future counseling, therapy, psychiatric care]
__I have gone to monthly sessions for counseling due to fears I have developed as a result of the crime. Each session costs $25, and I have been to 12 sessions. I intend to continue for the next 12 months.__

AMOUNT OF COUNSELING/THERAPY EXPENSES:

$ __300.00__ (TO DATE: _of sentence_) (insert date of sentence)

$ __300.00__ (ANTICIPATED)

THIS CRIME AFFECTED ME PERSONALLY BY: [describe emotional injury, change in life-style, change in attitude, change in family/social relationships, hardships endured as a result of this crime] __Since the crime, I have not felt safe in my car. I cannot park in a parking garage and I distrust anyone who looks like they are watching me. I have had to change jobs, because I cannot stay outside after dark. This has disrupted my classwork at the local college. I am also suffering in my relationship with my family, because they do not understand my fears.__

THIS CRIME AFFECTED MY FAMILY BY: [describe emotional injury, change in life-style, change in attitude, change in family/social relationships]
__My family, especially my husband, has been severely affected by the crime. I always ask to be driven now with my injured hip I feel as if I am not safe. It is very stressful for them.__

I HAVE INCURRED EMPLOYMENT-RELATED LOSS: [include description of how this has affected your ability to earn a living, loss of job, wages, days, anticipated future loss]
__I have changed jobs due to the crime and lost my opportunities for promotion, since I do not feel safe to travel at night which was a requirement of the former job. I have lost at least $10,000 in salary per year.__

I AM/AM NOT ELIGIBLE FOR WORKMEN'S COMPENSATION. IF COVERED, I HAVE/ HAVE NOT APPLIED.

AMOUNT OF EMPLOYMENT EXPENSES:
$____15,000.____ (TO DATE: of sentence) (insert date of sentence)
$ 10,000. or more each year___ (ANTICIPATED)

I HAVE INCURRED PROPERTY-RELATED LOSS: [include description of property, damages or loss, cost to repair, replace loss]
My car was recovered abandoned and smashed beyond repair. Its value was $12,000. Also, all my valuables in the car were either stolen or ruined and I lost various music discs, files and other valuable items.

IS PROPERTY IN CUSTODY OF POLICE? Only the car and recovered items.

AMOUNT OF PROPERTY LOSS:
$ $13,000._____ (TO DATE: of sentence) (insert date of sentence)
$_____ (ANTICIPATED)

I HAVE INCURRED OTHER LOSS: [include description of other damages or loss]
____I have had to pay for transportation expenses until insurance replaced my car._____
_____
_____
_____

AMOUNT OF LOSS:
$ 340.00._____ (TO DATE: of sentence) (insert date of sentence)
$_____ (ANTICIPATED)

BEING A VICTIM OF A CRIME: [include your feelings about the criminal justice process, and how you feel about your role in this case]
Every day I experience flashbacks of that night. I feel it is a permanent part of me. I have a feeling that this will never end. The case has taken a long time to complete and this has delayed my ability to get on with my life. I am glad I had a victim advocate in the prosecutor's office to help me get through this.

_____
_____
_____
_____
_____
_____

ALTHOUGH THE JUDGE WILL MAKE THE DECISION ON THE APPROPRI-ATE SENTENCE I WOULD LIKE TO SEE THE OFFENDER BE SENTENCED TO: [include any or all of the following - PROBATION, RESTITUTION, JAIL OR PRISON, OTHER]
DESCRIBE ANY OTHER INFORMATION YOU WANT THE COURT TO CON-SIDER.

    I believe this person should pay for his crime at least as
 long as I have to live with it. He should not be free in
 society for a very long time to think about what he has done.
 I recommend at least 15 years.

To the best of my knowledge, the above information is true and correct. I under-stand that filing a claim for restitution does not affect my right to file a civil suit or apply for Crime Victim's Compensation.

_____
Rhonda Jones   *May 2, 2001*
Your Name   Date

Form E. Sample Civil Complaint
(Baby-sitter Abused Child)

IN THE NINTH CIRCUIT COURT, FOR JEFFERSON COUNTY
STATE OF COLUMBIA

C.D., by John Doe, as next friend)
and Guardian.)
                  Plaintiff,)
) Case No. _____
v.)
)
Susan Smith ,   Defendant.)

COMPLAINT

COMES NOW, the minor plaintiff above named, by her Parent , John Doe, and files this Complaint against the defendant, for the following:

1.   The plaintiff is C.D., a minor, and is the natural daughter of John Doe. Plaintiff resides at 123 Elm Street, Anytown, Columbia. The plaintiff was born on April 1, 1991.

2.   The plaintiff brings this action by and through John Doe, her parent, who resides at 123 Elm Street, Anytown, Columbia.

3.   The defendant is Susan Smith, and resides at 47259 Borden Road, Anytown, Columbia. The defendant was at all times relevant herein the baby-sitter of the plaintiff.

4.   At all times herein mentioned, the defendant was charged with the supervision, care, custody, and control of the minor plaintiff in her capacity as baby-sitter.

5.   On or about the end of July, 1996, the plaintiff's parents hired the defendant and delegated all of their duties as natural parents to the said "baby sitter" for those periods of time when the baby-sitter had care and control of the minor plaintiff.

6.   On August 14, 1996, while the minor plaintiff was in the sole custody and care of the defendant, the minor plaintiff was beaten about the face and body by defendant, sustaining severe, serious, and permanent injuries as more specifically hereinafter set forth.

7.   That the damages and injuries sustained by the minor plaintiff were caused and were the direct and proximate result of the intentional and negligent wrongful acts of the baby-sitter, specifically:

(a)   That the defendant did willfully and maliciously strike, beat, kick, and otherwise harm the plaintiff;

(b)   That the defendant was not competent to perform the duties of caring for the plaintiff and failed to exercise the requisite proper skill or experience;

8.   That by reason of the carelessness, recklessness, negligence, and intentional conduct of the defendant, the minor plaintiff sustained severe and serious injuries of a permanent nature, specifically:

(a)   Abrasions of the eyes, mouth, and ears;
(b)   Brain contusion;
(c)   Motor and visual problems.

9.   That as a result of said injuries, the plaintiff was required to receive medical care and treatment, x-rays, hospitalization, and other proper and necessary things in an effort to restore her health and will, by reason of said injuries, be required to undergo additional and similar medical care and treatment for the rest of her life.

10.   That as a result of said injuries and the consequences thereof, the plaintiff has suffered great physical pain and agony, inconvenience, and mental anguish; and will continue to suffer considerable pain and agony, inconvenience, and mental anguish in the future for the rest of her life.

WHEREFORE, plaintiff (C.D.), brings this action against the defendant to recover damages for a sum in excess of $ 250,000.00 Dollars.

_____

[SIGNATURE]

INDEX

Your #1 Source for Real World Legal Information...

SPHINX® PUBLISHING

An Imprint of Sourcebooks, Inc.®

- Written by lawyers
- Simple English explanation of the law
- Forms and instructions included

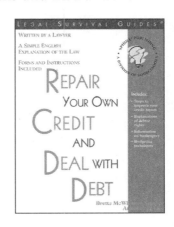

WINNING YOUR PERSONAL INJURY CLAIM, 2ND ED.

If you have been the victim of an accident of personal injury, you deserve compensation. This book includes an overview of the litigation process as well as sample letters for dealing with an insurance claim.

280 pages; $24.95;
ISBN 1-57248-138-2

REPAIR YOUR OWN CREDIT AND DEAL WITH DEBT

Learn how to keep creditors from harassing you, reduce your monthly payments and lower your debt. This guide also provides budgeting tips and sample letters to creditors, credit bureaus, and credit reporting agencies.

192 pages; $18.95;
ISBN 1-57248-149-8

THE MOST VALUABLE PERSONAL LEGAL FORMS YOU'LL EVER NEED

This book allows you to easily tailor your own simple contracts, forms, and agreement. Complete with step-by-step instructions and the forms you will need to create a will, pre-marital and divorce agreements, roommate agreements, and more!

272 pages; $24.95;
ISBN 1-57248-130-7

See the following order form for books written specifically for California, Florida, Georgia, Illinois, Massachusetts, Michigan, Minnesota, New York, North Carolina, Ohio, Pennsylvania, and Texas!

What our customers say about our books:

"It couldn't be more clear for the lay person." —R.D.

"I want you to know I really appreciate your book. It has saved me a lot of time and money." —L.T.

"Your real estate contracts book has saved me nearly $12,000.00 in closing costs over the past year." —A.B.

"...many of the legal questions that I have had over the years were answered clearly and concisely through your plain English interpretation of the law." —C.E.H.

"If there weren't people out there like you I'd be lost. You have the best books of this type out there." —S.B.

"...your forms and directions are easy to follow." —C.V.M.

Sphinx Publishing's Legal Survival Guides
are directly available from the Sourcebooks, Inc., or from your local bookstores.
For credit card orders call 1–800–432–7444, write P.O. Box 4410, Naperville, IL 60567-4410,
or fax 630-961-2168

SPHINX® PUBLISHING'S NATIONAL TITLES

Valid in All 50 States

LEGAL SURVIVAL IN BUSINESS

How to Form a Delaware Corporation from Any State	$24.95
How to Form a Limited Liability Company	$22.95
Incorporate in Nevada from Any State	$24.95
How to Form a Nonprofit Corporation	$24.95
How to Form Your Own Corporation (3E)	$24.95
How to Form Your Own Partnership	$22.95
How to Register Your Own Copyright (3E)	$21.95
How to Register Your Own Trademark (3E)	$21.95
Most Valuable Business Legal Forms You'll Ever Need (2E)	$19.95
Most Valuable Corporate Forms You'll Ever Need (2E)	$24.95

LEGAL SURVIVAL IN COURT

Debtors' Rights (3E)	$14.95
Grandparents' Rights (3E)	$24.95
Help Your Lawyer Win Your Case (2E)	$14.95
Jurors' Rights (2E)	$12.95
Legal Research Made Easy (2E)	$16.95
Winning Your Personal Injury Claim (2E)	$24.95

LEGAL SURVIVAL IN REAL ESTATE

How to Buy a Condominium or Townhome	$19.95
How to Negotiate Real Estate Contracts (3E)	$18.95
How to Negotiate Real Estate Leases (3E)	$18.95

LEGAL SURVIVAL IN PERSONAL AFFAIRS

Cómo Hacer su Propio Testamento	$16.95
Guía de Inmigración a Estados Unidos (2E)	$24.95
Cómo Solicitar su Propio Divorcio	$24.95
How to File Your Own Bankruptcy (4E)	$21.95
How to File Your Own Divorce (4E)	$24.95
How to Make Your Own Will (2E)	$16.95
How to Write Your Own Living Will (2E)	$16.95
How to Write Your Own Premarital Agreement (2E)	$21.95
How to Win Your Unemployment Compensation Claim	$21.95
Living Trusts and Simple Ways to Avoid Probate (2E)	$22.95
Most Valuable Personal Legal Forms You'll Ever Need	$24.95
Neighbor v. Neighbor (2E)	$16.95
The Nanny and Domestic Help Legal Kit	$22.95
The Power of Attorney Handbook (3E)	$19.95
Repair Your Own Credit and Deal with Debt	$18.95
Social Security Benefits Handbook (2E)	$16.95
Unmarried Parents' Rights	$19.95
U.S.A. Immigration Guide (3E)	$19.95
Your Right to Child Custody, Visitation and Support	$22.95

Legal Survival Guides are directly available from Sourcebooks, Inc., or from your local bookstores.
Prices are subject to change without notice.

For credit card orders call 1–800–432–7444, write P.O. Box 4410, Naperville, IL 60567-4410
or fax 630-961-2168

SPHINX® PUBLISHING ORDER FORM

BILL TO:		SHIP TO:		
Phone #	Terms	F.O.B. Chicago, IL	Ship Date	

Charge my: ☐ VISA ☐ MasterCard ☐ American Express

☐ **Money Order or Personal Check**   Credit Card Number   Expiration Date

Qty	ISBN	Title	Retail	Ext.	Qty	ISBN	Title	Retail	Ext.
		SPHINX PUBLISHING NATIONAL TITLES			____	1-57071-345-6	Most Valuable Bus. Legal Forms You'll Ever Need (2E)	$19.95	____
____	1-57248-148-X	Cómo Hacer su Propio Testamento	$16.95	____	____	1-57071-346-4	Most Valuable Corporate Forms You'll Ever Need (2E)	$24.95	____
____	1-57248-147-1	Cómo Solicitar su Propio Divorcio	$24.95	____	____	1-57248-130-7	Most Valuable Personal Legal Forms You'll Ever Need	$24.95	____
____	1-57071-342-1	Debtors' Rights (3E)	$14.95	____	____	1-57248-098-X	The Nanny and Domestic Help Legal Kit	$22.95	____
____	1-57248-139-0	Grandparents' Rights (3E)	$24.95	____	____	1-57248-089-0	Neighbor v. Neighbor (2E)	$16.95	____
____	1-57248-087-4	Guía de Inmigración a Estados Unidos (2E)	$24.95	____	____	1-57071-348-0	The Power of Attorney Handbook (3E)	$19.95	____
____	1-57248-103-X	Help Your Lawyer Win Your Case (2E)	$14.95	____	____	1-57248-149-8	Repair Your Own Credit and Deal with Debt	$18.95	____
____	1-57071-164-X	How to Buy a Condominium or Townhome	$19.95	____	____	1-57071-337-5	Social Security Benefits Handbook (2E)	$16.95	____
____	1-57071-223-9	How to File Your Own Bankruptcy (4E)	$21.95	____	____	1-57071-399-5	Unmarried Parents' Rights	$19.95	____
____	1-57248-132-3	How to File Your Own Divorce (4E)	$24.95	____	____	1-57071-354-5	U.S.A. Immigration Guide (3E)	$19.95	____
____	1-57248-100-5	How to Form a DE Corporation from Any State	$24.95	____	____	1-57248-138-2	Winning Your Personal Injury Claim (2E)	$24.95	____
____	1-57248-083-1	How to Form a Limited Liability Company	$22.95	____	____	1-57248-097-1	Your Right to Child Custody, Visitation and Support	$22.95	____
____	1-57248-099-8	How to Form a Nonprofit Corporation	$24.95	____			**CALIFORNIA TITLES**		
____	1-57248-133-1	How to Form Your Own Corporation (3E)	$24.95	____	____	1-57248-150-1	CA Power of Attorney Handbook (2E)	$18.95	____
____	1-57071-343-X	How to Form Your Own Partnership	$22.95	____	____	1-57248-151-X	How to File for Divorce in CA (3E)	$26.95	____
____	1-57248-119-6	How to Make Your Own Will (2E)	$16.95	____	____	1-57071-356-1	How to Make a CA Will	$16.95	____
____	1-57071-331-6	How to Negotiate Real Estate Contracts (3E)	$18.95	____	____	1-57248-145-5	How to Probate and Settle an Estate in California	$26.95	____
____	1-57071-332-4	How to Negotiate Real Estate Leases (3E)	$18.95	____	____	1-57248-146-3	How to Start a Business in CA	$18.95	____
____	1-57248-124-2	How to Register Your Own Copyright (3E)	$21.95	____	____	1-57071-358-8	How to Win in Small Claims Court in CA	$16.95	____
____	1-57248-104-8	How to Register Your Own Trademark (3E)	$21.95	____	____	1-57071-359-6	Landlords' Rights and Duties in CA	$21.95	____
____	1-57071-349-9	How to Win Your Unemployment Compensation Claim	$21.95	____			**FLORIDA TITLES**		
____	1-57248-118-8	How to Write Your Own Living Will (2E)	$16.95	____	____	1-57071-363-4	Florida Power of Attorney Handbook (2E)	$16.95	____
____	1-57071-344-8	How to Write Your Own Premarital Agreement (2E)	$21.95	____	____	1-57248-093-9	How to File for Divorce in FL (6E)	$24.95	____
____	1-57248-158-7	Incorporate in Nevada from Any State	$24.95	____	____	1-57071-380-4	How to Form a Corporation in FL (4E)	$24.95	____
____	1-57071-333-2	Jurors' Rights (2E)	$12.95	____	____	1-57248-086-6	How to Form a Limited Liability Co. in FL	$22.95	____
____	1-57071-400-2	Legal Research Made Easy (2E)	$16.95	____	____	1-57071-401-0	How to Form a Partnership in FL	$22.95	____
____	1-57071-336-7	Living Trusts and Simple Ways to Avoid Probate (2E)	$22.95	____	____	1-57248-113-7	How to Make a FL Will (6E)	$16.95	____
							Form Continued on Following Page	**SUBTOTAL**	

To order, call Sourcebooks at 1-800-432-7444 or FAX (630) 961-2168 (Bookstores, libraries, wholesalers—please call for discount)

Prices are subject to change without notice.

SPHINX® PUBLISHING ORDER FORM

Qty	ISBN	Title	Retail	Ext.
_____	1-57248-088-2	How to Modify Your FL Divorce Judgment (4E)	$24.95	_____
_____	1-57248-144-7	How to Probate and Settle and Estate in FL (4E)	$26.95	_____
_____	1-57248-081-5	How to Start a Business in FL (5E)	$16.95	_____
_____	1-57071-362-6	How to Win in Small Claims Court in FL (6E)	$16.95	_____
_____	1-57248-123-4	Landlords' Rights and Duties in FL (8E)	$21.95	_____

GEORGIA TITLES

Qty	ISBN	Title	Retail	Ext.
_____	1-57248-137-4	How to File for Divorce in GA (4E)	$21.95	_____
_____	1-57248-075-0	How to Make a GA Will (3E)	$16.95	_____
_____	1-57248-140-4	How to Start a Business in Georgia (2E)	$16.95	_____

ILLINOIS TITLES

Qty	ISBN	Title	Retail	Ext.
_____	1-57071-405-3	How to File for Divorce in IL (2E)	$21.95	_____
_____	1-57071-415-0	How to Make an IL Will (2E)	$16.95	_____
_____	1-57071-416-9	How to Start a Business in IL (2E)	$18.95	_____
_____	1-57248-078-5	Landlords' Rights & Duties in IL	$21.95	_____

MASSACHUSETTS TITLES

Qty	ISBN	Title	Retail	Ext.
_____	1-57248-128-5	How to File for Divorce in MA (3E)	$24.95	_____
_____	1-57248-115-3	How to Form a Corporation in MA	$24.95	_____
_____	1-57248-108-0	How to Make a MA Will (2E)	$16.95	_____
_____	1-57248-106-4	How to Start a Business in MA (2E)	$18.95	_____
_____	1-57248-107-2	Landlords' Rights and Duties in MA (2E)	$21.95	_____

MICHIGAN TITLES

Qty	ISBN	Title	Retail	Ext.
_____	1-57071-409-6	How to File for Divorce in MI (2E)	$21.95	_____
_____	1-57248-077-7	How to Make a MI Will (2E)	$16.95	_____
_____	1-57071-407-X	How to Start a Business in MI (2E)	$16.95	_____

MINNESOTA TITLES

Qty	ISBN	Title	Retail	Ext.
_____	1-57248-142-0	How to File for Divorce in MN	$21.95	_____

NEW YORK TITLES

Qty	ISBN	Title	Retail	Ext.
_____	1-57248-141-2	How to File for Divorce in NY (2E)	$26.95	_____
_____	1-57248-105-6	How to Form a Corporation in NY	$24.95	_____
_____	1-57248-095-5	How to Make a NY Will (2E)	$16.95	_____
_____	1-57071-185-2	How to Start a Business in NY	$18.95	_____
_____	1-57071-187-9	How to Win in Small Claims Court in NY	$16.95	_____

Qty	ISBN	Title	Retail	Ext.
_____	1-57071-186-0	Landlords' Rights and Duties in NY	$21.95	_____
_____	1-57071-188-7	New York Power of Attorney Handbook	$19.95	_____
_____	1-57248-122-6	Tenants' Rights in NY	$21..95	_____

NORTH CAROLINA TITLES

Qty	ISBN	Title	Retail	Ext.
_____	1-57071-326-X	How to File for Divorce in NC (2E)	$22.95	_____
_____	1-57248-129-3	How to Make a NC Will (3E)	$16.95	_____
_____	1-57248-096-3	How to Start a Business in NC (2E)	$16.95	_____
_____	1-57248-091-2	Landlords' Rights & Duties in NC	$21.95	_____

OHIO TITLES

Qty	ISBN	Title	Retail	Ext.
_____	1-57248-190-0	How to File for Divorce in OH (2E)	$24.95	_____

PENNSYLVANIA TITLES

Qty	ISBN	Title	Retail	Ext.
_____	1-57248-127-7	How to File for Divorce in PA (2E)	$24.95	_____
_____	1-57248-094-7	How to Make a PA Will (2E)	$16.95	_____
_____	1-57248-112-9	How to Start a Business in PA (2E)	$18.95	_____
_____	1-57071-179-8	Landlords' Rights and Duties in PA	$19.95	_____

TEXAS TITLES

Qty	ISBN	Title	Retail	Ext.
_____	1-57071-330-8	How to File for Divorce in TX (2E)	$21.95	_____
_____	1-57248-114-5	How to Form a Corporation in TX (2E)	$24.95	_____
_____	1-57071-417-7	How to Make a TX Will (2E)	$16.95	_____
_____	1-57071-418-5	How to Probate an Estate in TX (2E)	$22.95	_____
_____	1-57071-365-0	How to Start a Business in TX (2E)	$18.95	_____
_____	1-57248-111-0	How to Win in Small Claims Court in TX (2E)	$16.95	_____
_____	1-57248-110-2	Landlords' Rights and Duties in TX (2E)	$21.95	_____

SUBTOTAL THIS PAGE _____

SUBTOTAL PREVIOUS PAGE _____

Shipping — $5.00 for 1st book, $1.00 each additional _____

Illinois residents add 6.75% sales tax _____

Connecticut residents add 6.00% sales tax _____

TOTAL _____

To order, call Sourcebooks at 1-800-432-7444 or FAX (630) 961-2168 (Bookstores, libraries, wholesalers—please call for discount)
Prices are subject to change without notice.